I went to the woods because I wished to live deliberately, to front only the essential facts of life, and see if I could not learn what it had to teach, and not, when I came to die, discover that I had not lived.

Henry David Thoreau, *Walden*

Life isn't about money. It's about God. It's about love. It's about family and relationships. It's about personal evolution, learning and growth.

Richard Paul Evans,
The Five Lessons I Learned From a Millionaire

Jack's Farm

Joan Levy Earle

Published by Creative Bound Inc.
Box 424
Carp, Ontario Canada K0A 1L0
(613) 831-3641
www.creativebound.com

ISBN 0-921165-87-0
Printed and bound in Canada

Book design by Wendelina O'Keefe

Library and Archives Canada Cataloguing in Publication

Levy-Earle, Joan, 1944-
Jack's farm / Joan Levy Earle.

ISBN 0-921165-87-0

1. Levy-Earle, Joan, 1944- --Marriage. 2. Earle, Jack--Marriage.
3. Authors, Canadian (English)--20th century--Family relationships.
4. Authors, Canadian (English)--20th century--Biography. I. Title.

PS8573.E967Z468 2006 C818'.5409 C2005-907548-1

This book
is dedicated
to
Arianna Joy Earle,
first grandchild of
Grampa Jack,
that she might
know him better.

Cover photo:
the entrance to
Jack's Farm

Contents

Prologue

"If you ever write a story about this house, I think I have found the perfect title," Jack said. It was Saturday night, and I had just settled into a visit to the farm to spend the weekend with my husband. We were sitting at the dining room table, with the candles burning, just about to devour our usual Saturday-night meal of a pre-cooked barbecued chicken from the nearby mini-mart, while waiting for the start of the "Prairie Home Companion" on Vermont's National Public Radio. Without electricity, we had quickly learned to love the battery-operated radio, and Garrison Keillor's show provided us with some good skits and, frequently, some stimulating Cajun music. "Guy Noir, Private Eye" was one of Jack's favorites.

It's a takeoff on the old radio show "Boston Blackie," well-written and often hilarious.

That evening Jack handed me a piece of paper from his memo pad that carried the words: *The House That Time Forgot.*

"It's an appealing title," was my immediate response. That little scrap of paper sat for several months in the midst of the clutter of our odds and ends tray on the kitchen table. I found it again recently and recalled that evening when I received it from my husband.

It is now almost one year later, and the time has come to tell the story—the story of a dream that came true, a desire of the heart that was granted. I see very clearly now, too, that this is a story of married love, a love that was fulfilled in the house that time forgot.

The House That Time Forgot

It seems fitting to begin this story as a fairy tale because any time that a dream comes true it seems destined, and therefore has an ethereal quality to it.

Once upon a time, a young Bell Canada repairman was called to a house in the bush to fix an out-of-service telephone. He did the job, and went home and shared with his wife the news that he had just visited an old farmhouse where an elderly lady was living without power or running water. The young man returned to this secluded spot and got permission from the owner to hunt grouse on her property.

During one of his later visits, he thought perhaps the mistress of the house had died. He didn't see any activity and the place appeared abandoned. It was very late in the fall of the year, and as he approached the house, he spotted small footprints in the freshly fallen snow. Then he saw her—dear little Hattie with her single-toothed smile of recognition. He was happy to report to his family that evening that the little lady who lived down the long lane alone, was still alive.

Several years passed and he saw the obituary announcing Hattie's passing. He clipped the announcement from the paper and kept it in the top drawer of his dresser. That was probably the day that "the house that time forgot" became the desire of Jack Earle's heart.

Until Hattie's death, Jack had never really expressed any interest in buying the property. Now, I could tell by how often he spoke of the place that his interest in this property in the middle of nowhere had taken on great significance. He was a quiet man who kept many of his thoughts and dreams to himself until he felt the time was right.

So this is the story of Hattie's farm, which became Jack's farm in 1996. And it is my story, too, because I am on my way to becoming the next old lady who lives down the lane.

The first time we visited this property in the late spring of 1994, Jack parked the truck about a quarter of a mile away. You couldn't see the house for the trees. We had inquired at the next-door neighbors, the Dewar family, to ask about the passing of Hattie and if the property had been sold yet. We learned that it hadn't and we were given a contact name. Hattie's cousin, Clarence Fiske, who spent the summers in Williamstown, was the executor of her estate, and we agreed that we would visit him at the first opportunity.

We drove to the bottom of the lane and walked around the closed gate that said "No Trespassing." I felt like an intruder, although knowing that Jack was interested in purchasing the property made it seem a little more proper. Besides, I reminded myself, Jack and Hattie were old friends.

The canopy of trees, now in full leaf, welcomed us, but as we got closer, I saw the tired grey farmhouse and we decided to stop at the foot of the small hill. The overgrown shrubs and grass seemed to be helping to protect the house from the elements. Despite the overgrowth, the farm had an appealing laneway, with the leaning boughs creating a cathedral-like appearance. Some of the mature oak trees towered to heights that spoke of a couple of hundred years of history, which gave them a lifespan that matched the age of the property.

Belden's Atlas of 1879 states that this land was settled by Alex Macdonald. Mr. Macdonald passed away in 1895, leaving the property to his adopted son, Fred Cheeseman, Hattie's father. Fred was a "home boy." Orphaned in England, he had been invited to come to Canada to live with the Macdonald family to be raised as their son. The Macdonalds had only daughters, and no doubt Mr. Macdonald knew that a son would be important to carry on the family farming tradition. In his will, Mr. Macdonald stated that Fred Cheeseman was required to build a separate home for his unmarried sister, should she desire to live on her own. It is possible that this house was actually built, as there is a sixteen- by eighteen-foot house just north and east of the property, with a separate laneway running adjacent to that section of the property. It sits on the ten acres of land that is only one field wide, and possibly could have been severed if there had been a desire to do so.

That day, I recall, there was such sadness to the appearance of the larger clapboard house because every window had been broken over the six years that it had been abandoned. Out back we noticed that what must have been a garden at one time was now a forest of small maple and rock elm trees. The weather-beaten wood seemed to be crying out for a coat of fresh paint to cover its aging greyness. There was a piece of tin missing from the roof of the drive shed, and waist-high refuse blocked the steps that led into the house at the summer kitchen door. Later, it would take two days of filling garbage bags full of empty tin cans and baling twine, newspapers and old feed and flour burlap bags to discover that there was a cement floor underneath.

There were several small outbuildings on the property that at one time may have been used to house chickens and pigs. The remnants of two square log buildings seemed to indicate that the first settlers had used these for shelter until the main house was built. A machine shed whose supporting beams had broken under the weight of dozens of years of winter snow sat just southeast of the house. Directly behind it stood a double barn, where the dairy cows had been milked and the farm operation undertaken. There was a date inscribed in the cement near the narrow door, which would have been the farmer's main entrance. It said 1904, and we could only surmise that this was the date when the first milking operations had begun. There were approximately a dozen stalls for cows, and four horse stalls that were situated in the next section of the barn. Stacks of old straw bales and a haymow still full of hay gave the barn an eerie feeling, as if someone had been using the building recently.

I remarked to Jack that it was too bad we didn't know of a movie company that wanted to film the story of a nineteenth century farmer because our non-electrified barn could have provided an authentic background setting. There were still a few farm implements inside, as well as an ancient hay wagon and an old saw that had to be powered by a tractor. Bags and bags of baling twine, as well as a brightly painted grain separator, sat waiting to be put to use.

Jack and I already owned property on a nearby country road. We had acquired it eight years earlier, and had even purchased house plans for a passive solar home we saw featured in *Harrowsmith* magazine that would make a perfect retirement setting. He always avoided the subject of when we might build this 'dream home,' and when the county decided to pave the road beside this property, his comment that "civilization was getting too close for his future lifestyle" was telling.

Now, as we stood staring at this two-storey, weather-beaten clapboard house, I said, "If you want this house, then we'll just put it all in God's hands."

A decade earlier, we had purchased an old building and stationery business in downtown Cornwall. Our lack of cash flow at that time and the owner's reluctance to budge from his asking price, had prompted Jack and I to "put it all in God's hands." In an act of faith at the time, I had slid a miraculous medal down the side of the old Kyte Building—an act I believe helped the owner change his mind and accept our offer. In the ensuing years, the stationery business had given us a living and the apartment upstairs had given us a home.

It was now May 1994, and I once again knelt down and planted a medal, this time in the ground beside a large oak tree across the lane from the old farmhouse. I said a prayer, and Jack bowed his head to join me in this new act of faith. Two more years would pass before the property became ours.

We officially named the property Golden Oaks Farm, but I later put a hand-painted sign at the entrance of the laneway announcing to all who drove in that this was "Jack's Farm." After all, he had discovered and fallen in love with the property many years before and he had always called it "Hattie's Place," so giving it the day-to-day name of "Jack's Farm" seemed entirely appropriate.

For a solitary soul who enjoyed his own company, this farm was idyllic. The property stretched one hundred and ten acres down a gravel road that was unmaintained past our lane entrance. Across the road were a couple of hundred acres of uninhabited bush, and bordering our property were several hundred acres of government bush. South of the property sat another neighbor's bush with a small creek running through it. Jack used to tell his friends that he was the caretaker of nearly seven hundred acres of "wild country" where the deer and the moose roamed freely, and a few grouse could be found, where the coyotes howled early in the spring and the turkey vultures returned each year to nest in his barn. Southeast of the property, a heronry had been established and played host to nearly thirty nests for the great blue heron.

There are old-growth trees still standing on the property. Some of them are oak, maple and elm and could be over two hundred years old. When Jack discovered a cedar grove on the southeast portion of the acreage, he nicknamed it "the Emily Carr Forest." Those cedars, well over a hundred years old, have exposed roots and are reminiscent of the West Coast sketches created by this famous Canadian painter. Some of them tower tall enough to block out the afternoon sun.

One of the tallest elms, quite near to the main farmhouse, has recently died and will need to be cut down. It is always so sad to have to fell a tower of strength that has been providing shade on the property for centuries. The birds love to sit high up on the limbs, and the squirrels have an unlimited number of places to hide their nuts and exercise their legs. Jack often said that watching the red squirrels scurrying all over the big trees reminded him of monkeys in the jungle—they seemed to fly from limb to limb fearlessly.

The house itself has been referred to as a virgin because it was never wired or plumbed. The term implies unspoiled and primitive, and I know of only one other in our county that has no hydro. There is a special charm to a house without buzzing, humming or other noises that come from pipes and power. There is no gurgling of a refrigerator, no hum of a furnace and no knocking of pipes. You can almost hear your heart beating at night when you crawl under the covers. Of course, the absence of streetlights offers a multitude of stars to observe on clear evenings, and a moon that shines so brightly that it provides light to make it easier to find the outhouse.

The purchase of a virgin house required that we build an outhouse as soon as possible. Interestingly, there was no outhouse when we bought the property. I suspect there might have been at one time, but for so many years Hattie lived alone with her two dogs and she likely was content to use a commode pot under her bed and keep life as simple as possible for herself. She was a very slight woman who apparently lived on a meager diet of porridge, soup and the odd can of ham. The last years of her time at the farm, Hattie had placed a little wooden bed, the size of an army cot, in the corner of the dining room, where her pot-bellied stove provided her only source of heat. The stove's small opening required that her logs be of a specific size in order to fit inside.

I remember Jim Dewar telling us of the night Hattie called in a panic for help. One of her logs had gotten stuck in the opening of the stove and she couldn't close the lid. I also recall the story of the time she froze her toes, and her neighbor Carolee had to rush her to the hospital. The result of that experience changed Hattie's final years. Her foot had to be amputated because gangrene had set in, and so she went directly to a nursing home and never returned to her beloved farmhouse. For Hattie, her new life at The Manor meant television, running water, showers, nourishing meals and some companionship. Her last four years, until she died at ninety-four, must have been luxurious compared to the daily struggles she had endured at the farm.

When people visit our farmhouse, they are constantly remarking on the quiet spirit and peaceful presence in the house. A few visitors have been sitting at the dining room table and have suddenly started to cry. It was usually when they began speaking about their inner feelings regarding life and love. At those times we felt privileged to share some of their deepest emotions. Perhaps they, too, were drawn a little closer to God by being in this unusual house. There is a strong sense of protection and peace as you sit at the dining room table, and we always believed that it came from the fact that Hattie shared her life here with God.

Hattie's father, Fred, died in 1957, having been a widower since 1944 when his wife Emily passed away. Hattie continued to live at the farm for the next thirty years, maintaining a few cows and chickens in the early years. She was a woman of faith and prayer, and could not have been afraid to live by herself after her father died. I tell people that she didn't live alone; she had the Holy Spirit as her constant companion. It has been suggested that she kept a diary, but no one has come forth to let me know if it still exists. What a joy it would be to share the contents of this journal!

Our purchase of this property wasn't easy since Hattie had not filed an income tax return for several years, and the estate was in trust to the provincial government until the necessary taxes could be paid. Even the price of the property was a little vague, with the executor of her estate suggesting that we make an offer that we thought reasonable. We knew what we could afford, and presented this offer to him. We heard nothing back, and after several weeks of frustration, we made contact again.

This time we were told that our offer had been low. We asked how low, and proceeded to offer an extra few thousand dollars, which was promptly accepted.

There had been no real estate office involved in the sale, but the executor was a lawyer himself, and we were confident that the deal would soon be closed. Much to our surprise, despite this fact, the transfer of the farm took nearly two more years before we had official possession of the property. The delay was due to a break in the succession of ownership when the deed was searched, and in order to get proper title, we needed a new deed through the court. That proved to be a challenge for our lawyer, but after another year of patience and prayer, and a determined legal representative, the deed was granted and we could finally announce that Jack had bought his farm.

Jack's dream property soon became my vision for the future. Sometimes I imagined that Hattie's spirit was still present in the house because I never felt isolated. When Jack would be working outside for several hours, I was content to putter, sweep, paint in my studio, or prepare the evening meal. There was a joy in my heart that I never felt in any other place we had lived. When I speak of a spirit, I am not referring to a ghostly apparition; I mean a spiritual presence, and a happy one at that. So often I felt that Hattie was smiling in Heaven, knowing that a man like Jack had bought her old farmhouse and was giving it new life. It was as though she had been blessing the two of us ever since we made the decision to purchase it. With its three tin ceilings and wide, decorative moldings, this must have been a very well-decorated place in its early life at the turn of the twentieth century. A hundred years later, it was being given a facelift.

I selected a Victorian style of wallpaper for the dining room, and papered two walls as soon as Jack had completed the sub-floor. People have asked me if it is the original wallpaper, as the pattern seems quite authentic. Naturally, the color is brighter, and on closer examination, one can tell it is new wallpaper.

A special little item left behind in an upstairs bedroom was a tattered copy of *The Upper Room*, a church publication. The date on the cover read February 1969, and because my daughter Lisa was born just a few weeks earlier in January 1969, the coincidence inspired me to christen my studio The Upper Room.

One of my earliest thrills was the discovery of this room over the summer kitchen. On our first visit inside the house, once we had permission to do some exploring, we found a door that led from the north bedroom. I asked Jack where it might lead, and of course, he said I should open it and find out. The room behind this door was the largest in the house. I was overjoyed that this space had the potential for a studio for me. Jack agreed to my adopting it that day, and once it had been cleaned up considerably, it became the space we used for spreading out the picnic lunches we brought from town. We even put in a daybed that doubled for both sitting and napping use.

At the time of our purchase, this big room had several horse harnesses stored in it. An old cistern and some fifty-year-old invoices still hung on a nail, which made us think that Fred Cheeseman had used this room as an office for his fence and gate business. There had probably been no one in the room for a decade or two. It needed a coat of paint badly, so that was an important project for our second summer of farm ownership. I volunteered to tackle the job, since this would be my future workplace, and bought a gallon of primer. The walls were made of unfinished plaster, so when I put my brush full of paint on the wall, it drank it as though it had been thirsty for too many years. Four gallons of primer later, the dirty grey colour had been improved to a greyish white and the overall appearance of the room changed. There is nothing like a coat of paint to give a room a lift, or provide new light for a darkened old house.

We moved a ten-foot trailer from our other

country property to Hattie's farm the first summer after we took possession and had sold those twenty acres. This tiny trailer provided us with the means of cooking a meal or boiling a kettle for coffee and tea. It was cosy, and offered a bit of a getaway for Jack if he needed a little rest away from the construction area.

A guest book had been an early purchase when we took possession of the farm. I loved to keep track of the visitors who stopped by, and the guest book served as a permanent record of the number of special occasions that were being shared in the house. My friend Mary, who was one of the first guests to visit the property, shared a cup of tea in the trailer with me in August 1996. Hers is a unique comment in the guest book because our old Brittany spaniel, Tessie, had deposited a little 'job' on the bench inside the trailer, and neither Mary nor I had noticed. Mary sat down and had a "shitty encounter," as she termed it. She was such a good sport about the incident, and I had forgotten to have her sign her name, so as she drove off she declared,

"Make a note that anytime you need another christening, you can give me a call!" It wasn't long after, that Tessie had to be put down, as she was now eleven and unable to walk or to function normally anymore. We buried her at the farm, beside two of our friend Sheryl's beloved cats.

After that first summer of gutting and cleaning, we felt that we were making progress, and the vision of our 'dream home' of the future was finally taking shape. A major glitch in our progress came about in January 1998 when the now-famous Ice Storm hit the area. After spending the previous summer clearing brush and small trees to tidy the property around the house, we now faced a maze of broken limbs strewn across the grounds. I still wonder why that didn't discourage Jack enough to give up the project, as he only had Sundays to work at cleaning up the mess. Undeterred, he cut and stacked that wood, and created a pile of about four cords' worth of pieces and branches between two trees not far from the drive shed. He said that not much could get done inside the house in the winter anyway.

One of his amusing comments to his friends in town was that maybe Ontario Hydro might think that his power poles had blown away, and replace them while they were fixing everyone else's poles. Naturally, it was just a joke, but ironically, many of our neighbors experienced for a couple of weeks the only life that Hattie had ever known: a house without power and toilet facilities. Of course, for our dairy-farming neighbors, doing their chores was most difficult, and they had to share generators to keep their operations going. It was a very trying period for them.

That January was also the time of Jack's cousin Bill's illness. A few weeks after the Ice Storm, Bill was hospitalized with pancreatic cancer. Jack's compassion knew no boundaries as he began to visit Bill twice a day, morning and evening, in the palliative care section of the hospital. When Bill died six weeks later, his widow, Lilias, gave Jack many of her husband's old hunting clothes and photos. I knew that Bill and Jack had been close, and I was so pleased that Jack was available to share time with

Bill during his final days. Jack's quiet nature gave strength to both Bill and his wife, and showed me another glimpse into the special qualities of my husband.

~

The plan for the renovations of the house and the timetable of when the work would be done was completely Jack's department. I did make one request, and to celebrate the beginning of the major changes, I gave Jack a card and gift for St. Joseph's feast day. St. Joseph is the patron saint of carpenters, and the gift appropriately was a book on the subject of renovations to old houses. In my card, I shared with Jack my daydream of a library, a special room that would be "the source of pleasure, knowledge and quiet." My note went on to say:

I am so proud that you are my husband. I have no idea how long our retirement time will be together, but I know that there is no one in the whole world

I'd rather spend it with than you.

Love and prayers, Joannie

P.S. The sun is shining. Go out to the farm and enjoy the day away.

What is interesting is that my suggestion of a library gave Jack the inspiration to make a major change in the layout of the house. From the original layout of three bedrooms, he changed the opening of the largest bedroom, put a closet where that opening had been, and took down the third bedroom wall. This allowed us to have a more spacious look to the area at the top of the main staircase, where three windows gave us lots of light in the library. As soon as the drywall was painted, Jack found some old hardwood in the barn and made me a five-shelf-high bookcase that looks as though it has always been there. Instead of taking time to strip the old planked floor, he painted it. There was just no time within his schedule to do otherwise. This made a big difference in freshening up the whole upstairs.

Finding the second staircase that had been built beside my studio room was another of the attractions for me when we first examined the house. I could see myself painting away in the studio, and then pausing to slip down into the kitchen for a coffee break. The extra stairs could also be an escape route in case of fire.

In June of 1999, the daybed that was being stored in my future studio room came in handy when some friends from Iron Mountain, Michigan, called and said that they were stopping by on their way to New England. We had met this couple in our bookstore and had been corresponding with them for several years. The news of our farm purchase had thrilled them, and when the opportunity came for them to be in our part of North America, we welcomed them as our first official overnight guests.

They were driving a camping van, but we invited them to stay in the house if they preferred. Carol and Stretch are both of a slight build so they fit together in the single daybed, and we slept in

Hattie's old iron bed. There were many laughs as we wined and dined on my father's gift of Lancaster perch. Stretch spent an afternoon helping Jack to begin the framing for the sunroom, and the grace we shared at mealtime included a special prayer for the renovation of the farm, and blessings on those who would visit us in the future.

Separate Worlds

We have learned to live with each other, accepting each other's edges and corners. Sometimes idiosyncrasies which used to be irritating become endearing, part of the complexity of a partner who has become woven deep into our own selves.

Madeleine L'Engle, *Two Part Invention: The Story of a Marriage*

Jack liked to measure life in terms of five-year or ten-year plans. When we bought the old bookstore, he talked to me about a five-year plan. I had been reluctant to get into the retail business, but agreed to the plan because we were going to share the running of the store together eventually. About a year after we opened The Sanctuary, I encouraged Jack to retire from his other full-time work and devote himself totally to renovating our living quarters over the store. Although the prudent thing to do financially would have been for him to continue at his job, it was a choice that we made on faith. With both of us giving our all to the endeavor, we believed that God would provide for our needs.

Leaving his day job gave Jack less stress, and in addition to spending the next few years upgrading the apartment, he began doing all the extras around the house like laundry and grocery shopping, and of course, the maintenance in the store. Our heritage building required weekly improvements and constant monitoring.

Jack did not enjoy cooking, so there were never meals ready at the end of my workday. But meal preparation was no significant effort, as Jack only liked plain meals of meat and potatoes, and after he started marathon running, he started to eat less of everything. He had lost about sixty pounds and didn't ever want to find them again. His food intake consisted of a hot chocolate for breakfast, followed by a coffee or two. He ate an apple for lunch, and had raw vegetables and a small portion of meat or fish for supper. On the weekends, he would let me cook him potatoes. He never ate Chinese, Italian, or any other exotic food. His favorite snack was a bag of potato chips, a luxury he indulged in on the weekend. He enjoyed a bottle of beer, which was usually followed by a rum and coke near bedtime. He drank a little more beer once he started his pioneer life. I am sure he burned a lot more calories with the heavy-duty, labor-intensive life at the farm.

I admired Jack's willpower and envied his ability to remain trim. He had been an avid tennis player in his thirties and I was secretly envious of the women who were privileged to share a tennis game with him. I decided to surprise him one summer during a family holiday in Lake Placid. I secretly took a few tennis lessons. When I announced that I would like to play a game with him, he was eager to do so, and pleased to learn of my interest in the sport. That game was disastrous, as he was much too advanced for my beginner status, and I hardly returned a ball. It became my first and last attempt to try to involve myself in his hobbies.

Jack's foray into marathon running started with a one-mile jog to the post office. He had put on weight during his return to college for his technology diploma, and he wanted to get the extra pounds off. He started running at the age of thirty and never stopped. His daily loop increased until it was a six-mile run, and he became interested in long-distance running. He trained for the first National Capital Marathon in Ottawa in 1975. He developed a shin splint early in the race, so his finish was delayed, and about five hours after he began, he eventually walked across the finish line at the Carleton University grounds. We had become very worried about him, wondering why he was taking so long.

In the same race four years later, Jack achieved his best time, finishing in the top ten percent of the field, at a time of two hours, fifty-six minutes, for the twenty-six-mile, three hundred and sixty-five-yard race. He just missed the medal cut-off for his age group, so the children and I bought him a trophy to record for posterity this amazing feat.

This race was held on Mother's Day at that time, and we all shared a roast beef feast with the other runners following the event. Jack inspired several other Cornwall runners to take part in the marathon, and he became a fixture in the community, as his running was usually done at the same time each day. There were only a few regular joggers in the city in those days, and people got accustomed to seeing him in his dark blue tracksuit and would often wave their encouragement. Jimmy Stokes, who was twice Jack's age and a source of inspiration, shared the Olympic Torch Run with him for the 1976 Montreal Olympics. They each ran a five-mile section along the St. Lawrence River in June of that year.

In addition to running, Jack skied cross-country, winning several medals for endurance and eventually completing the two-day Canadian Ski Marathon. The most exciting part of that event, he told me, was the stopover at the Château Montebello in Quebec. He fell in love with the two-storey-high stone fireplace and promised to take me there for a getaway weekend one day.

Jack had the habit of doing things quietly and methodically, taking his time to think things through before making any decision. His lifestyle was in sharp contrast to my spontaneous, impulsive nature. I learned after several difficult years of adjustment in our marriage that his was the better way of making decisions, yet I am sure he also appreciated my enthusiastic approach to life. They say that opposites attract. I think that happens because the two different personalities can complement and complete each other…once the maturing process has been established.

It took me almost twenty years to truly believe

that I had married the right man. When I was sixteen years old, I remember visiting a fortune teller who told me that I was going to marry a tall, dark, handsome man some day. I wasn't very impressed with her prediction, as I was madly in love with my first love at the time—a tall, fair-haired young man. I couldn't imagine ever meeting anyone else, let alone marrying him.

First love makes that kind of impression on you. You are absolutely positive that you can never be happier than you are at that moment, nor can you think of ever being more in love with anyone else. And that is how it should be. First love teaches you how to love with your whole heart and mind and soul.

For some people, first love becomes their only love, and high school sweethearts marry and live happily ever after. I didn't have the chance to meet Jack in high school because my father was transferred away from Cornwall and I only returned after I had spent my early twenties in Toronto. Besides, I was such a snob in those days that even if I had caught a glimpse of his handsome face with the crooked smile in grade ten or eleven, I would have ignored him. Jack was one of those "tech" guys, and I would only have dated guys who were academically inclined and heading off to university. How foolish I would have been, and how grateful I am that I only met Jack after I returned to my hometown and had matured.

I met Jack at my father's sporting goods store. It was a Friday night in early April of Canada's centennial year, 1967. I had been working late at the downtown studio where I taught baton twirling and did some artwork. I had moved back home from the big city of Toronto nine months before and was staying with my parents until I could accumulate a nest egg and afford a place of my own. The six years I had spent living in the exciting world of Toronto had taken all of my finances just to cover my expenses. I was also guilty of spending whatever I had in my pocket. When my pocket was empty, I did without, but when I had some extra, I loved to share it and celebrate life.

His dark hair and dark eyes attracted me the instant I spotted Jack chatting with the boys in the back room of the store. It was almost closing time, so I didn't have very long to flirt with him. Jack's interest in hunting had made him a regular customer in my dad's shop. My sister Diana knew him a little from having gone to the trap club with my dad, so she spoke to him while I just stared and drooled. I remember Dad introducing me to Jack, saying, "This is my oldest daughter, Joan."

All the way home in the car, I couldn't stop asking my father questions about Jack. I was sitting on the side of Dad's easy chair, still wanting to know more, when the phone rang. The caller was asking for me, and my prayers had been answered. It was Jack and he wanted to know if I would like to go out for a drink with him. I put on a red sweater and a black skirt that showed off my figure to its best advantage, and we went for a drive in his new car, coincidentally a red Volvo with black leather seats. It was a one-year-old demonstrator, the newest car he had ever owned, and he was very proud of it.

He took me to the Glendale Hotel, a popular eating spot along the river, and we sipped a few rum and cokes and got to know each other better. We even parked at his boathouse on the way home and shared a few passionate kisses. This man was not like anyone else I had ever met, and within a few weeks, I was head over heels in love with him.

I think Jack was also attracted to me, but like many women before me, I could hear wedding bells in my head and began to drop several hints about the possibility of a future together. I was twenty-two years old, a seemingly prime age for marrying, and didn't really have any other major plans for my future at that time. There was another man in the background, and he eventually became the catalyst for Jack and me to tie the knot. He was ten years older, lived in Toronto, and his personality was very different from Jack's.

Although Jack was sensitive and sincere, he always had a difficult time sharing his private and innermost feelings. His father, Lloyd, had died before Jack was five years old, and life had been very tough for him, his sister and his mom as they struggled to make ends meet. His mother was a talented seamstress and earned a few dollars from that in order to supplement a meager mother's allowance. They did survive and Jack learned quickly how to save his money a dollar at a time for something special. Although we admired his capability at being a saver, my family and I used to tease him later that he was a squirrel, hiding away little bits of money.

Jack and I dated on and off again all through the summer of 1967, and finally, around Thanksgiving, I told him that things didn't seem to be working out, so we might as well call it quits. In fact, I spent that Thanksgiving in Toronto visiting my other friend.

I was working in my dad's store doing some bookkeeping for him the Thursday after Thanksgiving when Jack walked in. When I saw him, my heart skipped a beat or two because the attraction was still there. He asked me if I would go out for a drink with him that night. I told him that might not be a good idea because things were over between us.

The breakup had been caused by a difference of opinion; I thought we were ready for marriage and he wanted to have more money saved before settling down. His practical side had won out, so we had agreed to end the relationship. There were other personality differences too, and it seemed too much of an impossible dream for us to make a life together.

One thing we did have in common was our faith. I had become a Roman Catholic just three weeks before meeting him. My conversion had been inspired by some Catholic friends I had met in Toronto. Jack was a churchgoer, and he once mentioned to me that he would not have even become serious about me had I not been of the same mind about our faith.

He said he wanted to take me out for a friendly drink that night because he was down in the dumps and just needed company. "Just two old friends out on a casual date," he said. I decided that it wouldn't do any harm and agreed. We drove down to the same quiet bar along the river where we had enjoyed our first date. This was the fall season, and the place was almost deserted. After two drinks, Jack said, very casually, that he would soon be having some vacation time, and would I be interested in going away with him somewhere for a few days. I responded by telling him that I wouldn't go away with a man unless I was married to him.

Jack's next line sounded glib to me: "Then why don't we get married?"

I said, "Sure, how about in three weeks?"

"Why not?"

The rest of our date was spent joking about the possibilities and it almost seemed as if we were play-acting. When he dropped me off at my house, I told him that I would give him my answer at noon the next day.

I wasn't sure he would even call me, but he did. His first words were, "Well, are we getting married?"

I answered, "Yes, and since I have to meet the priest to do some posters for him tonight, why don't you join me there and we can talk to him." I was calling his bluff, but my heart was beating louder than I had ever heard it beat, and I felt like I was on a merry-go-round, enjoying the ride and not wanting to get off.

We signed the papers that night, announced the news to my parents, and made plans for November 11, Remembrance Day. We were married at nine o'clock in the morning and honeymooned in Lake Placid. I chose a hot-pink lace suit, and my grandfather made my wedding cake. We entertained about thirty-five of our relatives and friends at my parents' home. My brother Eddy was the bartender, and the ironing board across the hallway made a perfect bar. Our attendants were Pat and Ed Cameron, the couple who lived next door to my parents, and who also happened to be my new godparents. They had encouraged my conversion to the Catholic faith and stood for me at my confirmation that same year. Jack had hoped that his best friend and cousin Bill would have been able to make it down from Pembroke to stand for him, but the quick planning of our nuptials made it impossible.

One of the greatest gifts I received from God by marrying Jack Earle was a loving mother-in-law named Lucille. Nanny Earle, as our children called her, was an accomplished seamstress, and one important way she helped me was by making costumes for my majorette school recitals every year. She also kept the children each Saturday when I was teaching my classes. We became very close friends, and she loved me unconditionally. She listened patiently to my whining whenever there were problems between Jack and me and, I am sure, prayed patiently for us and for our marriage.

In 1981, I decided to retire from my majorette school. It was a providential decision because that was the same year that Nanny died, and I could never have held an annual recital without her. She took such pride in seeing the students on stage, and she often told me that it gave her something special to look forward to each year. Her heart attack at age sixty-five took her from us much too soon, but I treasure the times we spent together on summer vacations and all the love she left behind in the hearts of her grandchildren and the friends she made by sharing her talent for sewing. I chose to be called Nanny Earle II in her memory, but as hard as I will try, I never expect to be the super-grandmother that she was.

One special legacy from her was finding her rosary beads and a little booklet on how to pray the rosary when I was cleaning out her dresser drawer after she died. That booklet taught me the mysteries of the rosary. I told her daughter Betty Ann the story of my introduction to the rosary when I presented her with her mother's rosary a few years later. No doubt those beads encouraged my sister-in-law as she battled several serious illnesses. Nanny Earle's life of faith continues to be an example to all of us.

After Nanny Earle's death, Rita, a first cousin to Jack's father, grew closer to us. Aunt Rita, as we called her, took us into her heart and filled the void of the friendship that I had known with Nanny Earle. She also prayed often for Jack and me and believed in our marriage. Her encouragement of my painting career helped keep the studio rent paid and she still holds the record for the most paintings purchased.

Strange as it may sound, while the rest of the world was getting prepared for "Y2K" and the prospects of a possible technology meltdown as the new millennium approached, Jack was spending his time as a pioneer and embracing the tasks of the nineteenth century. He was hard at work fixing up an old farmhouse that had no power or indoor plumbing. Thank God for the invention of generators as essential workmates so that power tools could be used.

In June of 2000, Jack and I had a short conversation in our store about the possibility of his moving to the farm permanently so that he could work at the renovations on a full-time basis. When I asked him what he thought of the idea, I think it took him a full minute to say yes. The condition to this arrangement was that our daughter Lisa would move back home to share the apartment with me. Her monthly offering of a few hundred dollars in rent money would allow us to have some raw material cash flow to begin our farmhouse renovation in earnest. She agreed and we began to make our plans. We would transfer most of our kitchen things and Jack's clothing to the farm. Lisa would become the main occupant, and I would rent a room in *her* apartment. That way our 'thirty something' daughter would continue to have her independence and enjoy the privacy of the apartment on weekends when mom visited dad at the farm.

This decision to free Jack from the store errands and day-to-day activity of our business required more effort from me in the store. However, business was slower and a new friend, Pat, had agreed to work part-time. With Judy, our present part-time lady, and now Pat, I knew I would manage. Our good friend Gordon, who was now retired, offered to visit the store a few times a week to take over the mail and the errands. Gordon was also a good ear for the lamentations of my missing Jack.

One of Jack's biggest concerns was how to keep an eye on his friend from his Bell days, Old Bob, as we called him, who was now in his eighty-sixth year. Jack used to arrange to meet Bob for coffee a few mornings a week just to keep an eye on him. Bob lived alone, and by meeting Jack, he had a reason to get out. Bob still enjoyed a cigarette, so the men met at one of the few coffee shops that permitted smoking.

When Bob's health began to deteriorate, Jack decided to call the Community Care nursing office to get some advice. He felt it was time to get Bob into a nursing home where he would receive three good meals each day, and twenty-four-hour supervision. God helped out, because there was an opening at a facility close to our store. I was able to walk there and visit once in awhile, especially on the days when Jack couldn't get into town.

I remember that we checked with Bob about his paperwork, and whether he had made out a will. He had one but it was not properly witnessed. We sold holograph wills in our stationery store, so we arranged for him to have a new will, properly witnessed. He died three days later on our wedding anniversary, and as Bob's daughter remarked: "My dad was special. He was born on Valentine's Day and died on Remembrance Day."

Jack had come to town that Saturday to pick me up, and decided to stop by and see Bob first, because he knew he was in frail health. Bob tried to say something to Jack, but then went to sleep. As Jack arrived at the store, the phone rang. It was the nursing home calling to say that Bob had just passed away. Jack told me later that he couldn't make out what Bob had been trying to say to him but later realized that Bob was trying to tell him that he was dying, and wanted to say goodbye.

There was no funeral home visitation at Bob's

request, but Bob's daughter, who lived several hundred kilometers away, wrote Jack a touching letter to thank him for all he had done for her father. For Jack, losing Bob was hard but also a blessing because his friend's quality of life had been lost.

Jack had also assisted Bob's son John to pass from this world to the next. John had become ill with terminal cancer, and when it came time for him to be hospitalized, Jack was a steady visitor. He had left his name as the person to contact when the end of John's life was in sight. When the hospital called, Jack offered to take Bob to say goodbye to his son, but Bob was too infirm to see him. Jack was there in his place when John died.

The living arrangement that we organized for our new lifestyle was that I would spend weekends and holidays at the farm, while Jack would live there full-time. Our Springer spaniel, Jessie James, couldn't express his delight in words, but he welcomed the move from the city apartment above a bookstore to the land of the free at the farm.

The decision for Jack to make this unusual move to the farm gave us hope that it might be a catalyst to finding a buyer for the retail business that we had been trying to sell for about two years. It took another two years before we would close the store, and another year before we would sell the building, but we felt that we had made a lot of progress by making this sacrifice. It was a sacrifice for both of us, but for Jack, who had to do the bull work, the major interior gutting and so on, this was a huge commitment. He traveled to town a couple of times a week for supplies and a shower. When he dropped by the apartment, he enjoyed putting a movie into the VCR and watching an hour or so of one of his favorites as a way of relaxing. One movie we bought was *Nobody's Fool*, and I later purchased a wallpaper border for the farmhouse kitchen that had a scene with two old pickup trucks on it because it would remind us of Paul Newman's old red truck in that movie.

The summer season was the most difficult for Jack from a practical standpoint because many of his foods needed to be kept cool. In winter, nature provided a giant cooler in the back shed, but by the end of May, you needed to use blocks of ice. Ice in a cooler is only a two- to three-day situation and that makes your choice of meals very limited. Jack didn't eat rice or canned vegetables. His staple winter food was Lipton's chicken noodle soup, and he became an expert at cooking it so that there was a pot full of noodles and very little broth. I don't recall any foods that he ate from a can, except salmon and the odd can of Spam, which he liked thinly sliced and fried. He would keep a supply of raw vegetables in the fridge in the back of the store, and picked up the extra ice packs for his cooler whenever he came to town. I am sure that our dog Jessie got Jack's hamburger patty a couple of times, if the weather got too warm and the meat began to turn. Not once did

Jack ever comment about the inconveniences. He always used to tell me that complaining serves no purpose, and after many, many years of married life, I finally learned how to follow his example.

Our son John, who was soon to be married, now nicknamed his father "Crazy Jack" because he had chosen to live without amenities. John became a frequent visitor to the farm and was available whenever there might be a problem too difficult for me to handle in the store. He admired his father's fortitude, and the pair went shopping for second-hand trail bikes that first summer so they could explore and enjoy the acreage. I wonder how John's fiancée Sarah viewed her future father-in-law when he made the decision to live out in the bush. A few of our friends teased Jack when they saw him in June 2001, dressed in his tuxedo at John and Sarah's wedding. "He cleans up well," they commented.

I was terribly lonely the first few months of our pseudo-separation. Jack had left the apartment physically, and although our daughter Lisa was now living with me, I missed his presence. I missed sipping a glass of wine on the patio after a long day in the store. I missed hearing him brush his teeth in the morning, or talking to him about the current events in the downtown area. All the little things that we take for granted about married life were the things I missed—even the frowns that might come over his face when I said the wrong thing or started to whine about my long day in the store.

Our weekends were special, however, and the adage that absence makes the heart grow fonder really did happen in our case. I saw my husband in his new role as a country dweller, and the joy on his face at each new achievement was worth the separation. He had already completed one renovation job of the apartment over our store many years before, but I had been too busy learning the stationery business to pay much attention to his daily routine of hammering and sawing. I was so busy that I didn't even mind the fact that I had no kitchen cupboards or counter-top area in the apartment for the first four years that we lived there. In lieu of cupboards, I used those handy archive boxes that you put files into at the end of the year. The kitchen had a laundry tub for dish washing, and an old wooden table that served as our counter.

I didn't entertain much those first few years, not so much because the apartment wasn't finished, but usually because the workload was so heavy that I often put in extra evening hours in the store. The only room that really mattered was the one that held the bed where I could finally flop at the end of the day. When you buy a ninety-nine-year-old business that needs to be rejuvenated, work has to be your main focus.

Sharing the Dream

Twilight calls,
The sun descends
And the earth is veiled in darkness;
No light, yet life persists,
And love grows,
With the essence of twilight time.

These words were a part of my poetic youth, a time when young love bursts forth. It's funny how forty-five years later, certain lines of poetry can still dance around in your head. One of my classmates from high school in New Brunswick, Ron Cole, wrote this short poem about twilight, and I recalled it recently when I was thinking about how much Jack loved the approach of the end of the day.

I only discovered this fact after he was living full-time at the farm. There was no power, and so in order to prepare our evening meal as the kitchen darkened, I would reach for the barbecue lighter that sat on the counter, and lean over to light our propane light on the wall just above the stove.

This propane light was the second one Jack had arranged to have installed in the house. The first one was hanging on the wall of the main living area near the staircase and was useful because it provided some light in the dining room, and near the stairs. The kitchen light was a surprise anniversary gift the fall of the year Jack had moved to the farm. It especially allowed me to get up at four in the morning to make bread.

I had tried to make the bread using candlelight as my source of light a few times, but it was very difficult. I couldn't imagine the monks in the monastery in centuries gone by who would have been doing this early morning chore as a portion of their sustenance. Perhaps they had better candle holders and eyes better adjusted to their semi-dark lifestyle.

On this particular day when I discovered Jack's fondness for twilight, he had interrupted my reaching over to light the kitchen light and inquired, "Is there any rush for supper?"

I hadn't noticed that he had been standing by the back window looking out at the trees south of the house, watching the fading sunlight dance on their darkening limbs. I joined him at the window, and paused for my first glimpse of this phenomenon that one cannot appreciate unless you are standing in a darkened house looking out at the sky, without streetlights.

Twilight spans a very short period, unlike a setting sun. It is that time just after the sun goes down and just before darkness descends. Of course, there is also a morning twilight that comes after dawn and just before sunrise.

"This is my favorite time of the day," Jack said.

Within ten minutes, he had walked over to the propane lamp above the stove, and silently lighted it. This was my cue that I could begin our supper preparations. Jack was a man of very few words. He spoke when it counted, and there were moments like this that I can never forget.

Before we were married, I wrote a poem for Jack and gave it the title "The Man in My Life." His love of nature had inspired it.

His every breath is filled with enthusiasm;
His sensitivity brightens for God's little creatures;
His intimate world is nature's wonderland.

A strong, determined man
Whose gentle soul
Reflects his depth of warmth.

I know his hands have tasted toil;
His eyes have witnessed sorrow;
His life has known a loneliness.
This man and all he is

Holds my fulfillment in his grasp;
His love is kind
And oh, how very good for me.

I didn't realize it then, but those words were prophetic because this man did fulfil my life in every sense. He taught me so much about nature and the true meaning of life, forgave my weaknesses, encouraged my artistic talents and quietly led our children to responsible adulthood.

For me, his silent strength was especially important early in my painting career. I had shown my work to a gallery owner who was also a framer. Jack had driven me out of town to pick up some paintings I had left there and I was optimistic that this gallery person would like my work and want to hang it in his shop. I left myself wide open for his criticism by inquiring if he might be interested in showing my paintings. His response was straightforward: "You are just an amateur." When I got to the car where Jack had been waiting patiently for me, I shared my disappointment.

As long as I live, I will be grateful for Jack's response to me that day: "That is only one man's opinion." His words of consolation prevented me from putting down my paintbrushes forever. I knew that I was quite amateurish in my approach at the time, but being a self-taught artist, I was continually exploring new ways of expression for my spirit. Instead of giving up, I decided then and there that I would show this gallery that I could one day become an accepted artist. To me acceptance meant that people would come to my exhibitions and purchase my work. And a few years later that began to happen when I held my own showings, even to the point of renting a suite at the Royal York Hotel and having an exhibition there. The joy of watching strangers coming to my show and wanting to buy a piece of my work gave me satisfaction and the desire to continue.

Jack often had to swallow hard and trust my instincts, because each time I staged one of those expensive out-of-town shows, I was taking a big financial risk. I am sure that some of those gambles were difficult for him to understand because the framing bill rose to the thousands of dollars on a couple of occasions. Thank God, I broke even and was able to return home with at least the frame money in hand.

My last Toronto show in 1987 at Cedar Ridge in Scarborough was the most successful and I was able to make a small profit from the sale of my paintings that year. By then I was becoming more of an established artist, and when it came time to purchase the Kyte store on Pitt Street the following year, my painting inventory helped to provide extra collateral to convince the bank that we should be approved for a loan to open The Sanctuary.

Jack was a good critic of my artwork. He had an eye for detail, and it would take over thirty years of married life for me to discover that he was an artist in his own right.

We sold mostly non-fiction books in our store, and one of our customers who enjoyed decoy books stopped by to browse. While Roy was in the store that day, he casually asked me if I had ever heard of a decoy carver named "Jack Earle." Roy was a serious decoy collector and he said that he had recently purchased a decoy by this local carver but that he had never heard of him previously. I told him that my husband was named Jack Earle and perhaps he was the person who had created this carving. The first opportunity I had I checked with Jack about the decoy. It was his work.

For years Jack had stored a couple of bags of decoys in the basement of our house, but I had never inquired as to their source. I was too busy being a mother to two young children and running a small business of my own to notice. I learned then that when Jack was about sixteen he was not able to afford the nicer style of wooden decoy for duck hunting, so he decided to make his own. They were successful carvings and he used them whenever he hunted on the St. Lawrence River. He had given a few of them away to relatives and friends in the past, so that must have been how this man had acquired a "Jack Earle carving." Later, when the customer brought the decoy to the store, he asked Jack to sign it for him, and I had a chance to admire it.

When this hidden talent of Jack's was revealed to me, I began to see him in a very different light. All the years I had known him, he had never boasted to me of this ability he had, but now I encouraged him to do a few new carvings, which he started to work on that winter. It was fascinating to discover this other side of a man I had lived with for so many years.

Purchasing the old bookstore had been Jack's idea and I had reluctantly agreed to the decision. I knew that retailing had been a part of my background, so operating the business should come naturally. In the beginning, I cried a river of tears over my inability to make a big profit in the stationery-bookstore business. I took my "manager's duties" very seriously and wanted to prove to my husband that I was doing a good job. Jack was inexperienced as a store proprietor and kept wondering where our profit was going. He didn't understand the reality of replenishing inventory, and we were paying down our mortgage more quickly than was required. During this learning period, my accountant, Brenda, became a closer friend, teaching me how to manage my cash flow and providing a listening ear.

It was only after the first eight years in business, when our daughter Lisa moved on from the family business to work elsewhere, that Jack started spending time in the store on a daily basis. He began to see that no matter how hard I worked, or how nice I was to customers, we were still dependent on the trade that came through the front door. He learned quickly and our teamwork evolved. He started to show me that he was proud of my effort, and we both became aware that our gifts were different, but they blended well.

Not long before this management changeover, I had poured my heart out to God and said, "I can't do this alone. I need You to fix this relationship," and within a few months, life really began to change. I learned to compliment my husband on the things he did well, and my improved attitude brought a positive response from him. We became better friends and our love deepened from the new respect we had for each other's abilities.

Operating the bookstore together gave me many new insights into Jack's wealth of knowledge. I often listened to him serving customers and discussing everything from the poetry of Edgar Allan Poe to how to read a topographic map. His interest in history, his experience fishing off the islands of the St. Lawrence River, and above all, his natural talent at fixing everything that might possibly go wrong in our hundred and sixty-year-old historic building all made me feel so fortunate to have married a Renaissance man.

In consideration of Jack's becoming a pioneer of the twenty-first century, I recall a quotation by

Charles Kingsley that holds true for everyone, no matter his age or station in life:

Thank God every morning when you get up that you have something to do which must be done, whether you like it or not. Being forced to work and forced to do your best will breed in you temperance, self-control, diligence, strength of will, content and 100 other virtues which the idle never know.

Having to tackle the chopping of wood in the fall to prepare for the winter months will give you a sense of necessary purpose. Getting up to let out a dog in the early morning hours and let in a cat that has been roaming and hunting the night before, makes you have to get out of bed.

A three-week-old kitten showed up on the porch steps of the farmhouse about a year after Jack had moved in. The little male tabby was weak, almost at the point of starvation, so Jack began to feed and care for him. He asked me to help name him, and since he had arrived on the Fourth of July, I suggested Sam, after 'Uncle Sam.' Sam adopted Jessie as a surrogate father and loved to curl up close beside him to share his body warmth. He grew into a great mouser, and once in awhile would drop a little dead chipmunk at the doorstep. Jack said that Sam left his night's catch at the door to show him that he was earning his keep.

Jack was a cat lover, and I think he preferred the quiet nature of Sam to Jessie's more rambunctious spaniel personality. He often remarked that Jessie was my dog, and indeed I looked forward to the welcome he gave me every weekend. He jumped, or should I say sprang, up at me when I got out of the truck. His style of greeting our visitors was in need of some discipline, so I began working on him and trying to teach him not to jump. He had a strong respect for Jack and never once tried the same stunt on him.

An old friend of Jack's, who knew him during his telephone repairman days, was living in St. Isidore, just fifteen minutes away. When Jack arrived permanently in the country, Doug called him almost weekly to check on him. It was good to see these two old friends reconnecting, and I think that Doug admired the tenacity of my husband to take on such a big project. We enjoyed going to Doug's home for the odd meal and a break away from the renovation project.

There are advantages to pioneer living. You travel to the laundromat to do your laundry and you fold it carefully because you will not be doing any ironing. There are no light bulbs to buy, and no electric bill to pay. There is no twice-yearly water tax bill, no kitchen appliances to dust like a microwave, food processor or toaster. You make your toast on the top of the stove and it tastes very good. The hand beater I picked up at my favorite antique store for two dollars mixes all of my cakes.

We did have a chance to watch a little television, as the first Christmas after Jack became a permanent resident at the farm, John purchased a five-inch black and white battery-powered television for his father. We soon learned that the batteries were expensive, so Jack created a car-battery solution and would bring that battery to town each week to recharge it at the store. Reception was amazing with about five channels coming in quite clearly. Our early-to-bed Saturday nights sometimes gave us a bonus of waking up around one in the morning to catch the late-night movie. On those nights I would grab an extra hour of sleep from three to four, before getting up early to make my whole-wheat bread.

Bread making was the fulfillment of one of my personal dreams. I found a short recipe in a monastery kitchen cookbook that required three risings, and molasses, honey and whole-wheat flour as the major ingredients. The first morning I made the bread, I noticed Jack was a little hesitant to try it. After all, he had spent the first thirty-two years of our marriage knowing me as a throw-it-together-quickly style of cook. He also had heard the story of my first bread-making adventure when I was a teenager. I had been staying with good friends in New Brunswick, helping with the kitchen chores while the lady of the house was having surgery. She had shown me once how to follow her recipe and to make her bread. While she was still in hospital, I thought I would surprise her husband and son with some homemade bread. That evening at dinner, her husband tasted the first slice of bread, and smiled politely and said, "Not too bad for your first attempt." The next morning he arose before me, and fed the chickens the three loaves of my bread that had become hard as a rock and not worth keeping. I never tried bread making again after that.

Jack loved bread, but tried to avoid eating it between the summer and winter solstice, knowing that bread and peanut butter were among his favorite foods. For me to announce that I was making bread the old-fashioned way was a major surprise. Fortunately, even the first batch of bread was good, and from that day on, we seldom purchased any other bread. My whole-wheat bread had no preservatives, but by keeping it cool, it had a seven-day shelf life.

I recall how excited I was to share the news with one of my customers the next day at the bookstore that I had made bread successfully the day before at our farm. The lady smiled and commented that bread making had become much easier since the invention of the bread machine. I then proceeded to inform her that I did not have power at the farm and had to make it the old-fashioned way, and it had taken three rises and four hours of preparation to accomplish this task. Only then did she realize why I was so excited about my accomplishment.

Our city friends were naturally curious about life as a pioneer and kept saying to Jack whenever they met him at the store, "So how is life in the bush?" He always smiled his little crooked smile and said things were fine. Many of them had never been out to the farm and the most-often-asked question was, "Got power yet?" Jack would say it was in the future plans, and leave it at that. It wasn't easy to explain that we were planning for solar power but it was a major investment. Once the building downtown was sold and the business closed or sold, whichever would come first, then we would have the cash to put in the solar power. We were looking at an investment of twenty thousand dollars, and even more than that if we chose to go the hydro-pole route. For now, it was not a major necessity and we were enjoying the novelty and the simplicity of "pioneer" life.

Part of Jack's daily routine was to get up with the sun and go to bed with the sun. Occasionally he would use the propane lamp in the kitchen to read in the early evening. For me one of the great pleasures from spring until fall was preparing our Sunday morning breakfast in the sunroom addition that Jack had completed the first year he lived in the house full-time. The walls of this room are lemon yellow and I chose a butterfly border to bring some extra gaiety to the atmosphere. With only Sundays to do any kind of work myself, it was a busy morning the day of John's thirtieth birthday when I was finishing the wallpapering just a half hour before the twelve guests arrived for our son's birthday lunch.

On a dull day, the sunroom had the most light with its full bank of windows. The view never bored us, especially in the spring when the birds began to return and entertain us with their various songs. The sun would rise differently each morning, and although the sunrise was only partially seen with the big old barn blocking the view to the east, there was still a joy at observing first light, and watching the clouds change colors. I saw first light alone with Jessie because Jack usually enjoyed a little extra sleep when I was with him on the weekends and could let the dog out.

The first floor of the house had two main rooms, a small entrance area, and a summer kitchen add-on. When we first visited the house and peeked into a window, Jack remarked to me that there was a tin ceiling in both the living and dining rooms. That seemed coincidental since our store also had a marvelous tin ceiling. The dining room ceiling had to be removed because there was a lot of damage from the burned pipes of Hattie's often-overheated pot-bellied stove. I thought the ceiling was going to be thrown away, so I was pleasantly surprised a year later when I discovered that Jack had taken the best of the tin ceiling squares and covered the now-smaller dining area with them. Part of this space was going to be our future downstairs bathroom, so the ceiling area had shrunk accordingly. He had recreated a complete pattern with the outside border and the inside tiles coming together to look the same, but smaller.

For our first Christmas after his move, my big surprise was the parlor ceiling now painted off-white, and two large red bows that he had placed on the outside of the farmhouse. The Christmas tree was a real one, picked from the southern portion of the property, and decorated with colorful round balls. It looked like a Charlie Brown tree and yet was the most beautiful one we had ever trimmed all the years of our marriage. It didn't even miss having lights on it because we had found some old-fashioned silver tinsel at our store and it shone in the sunlight. When I went upstairs, there was a smaller artificial tree in the library, where Jack had placed my presents. My plan was to go into town very early on Christmas morning to visit our children, and I had to learn a lesson that the woodstove needed to be fed every few hours, so our visit was going to be a short one.

The different seasons of the year offer different challenges for country dwelling. Jack anticipated the coming of the grouse season and would point out to me the sound of the drumming partridge as we took our early spring walks. Taking time to "smell the roses," or in his case, taking time for a walk on his hundred-acre retreat was a bonus at the end of September. He would pride himself when he got a September bird or two. The brush was always extra thick and it was never an easy trek through the long grass to reach the hedges where a partridge might be feeding.

Once he had moved from the city to Hattie's farm, Jack no longer faced the forty-minute drive to and from his favorite hunting retreat. When he became self-employed after buying the bookstore, he was always considerate of my needs over his hunting time, and if the store was busy he'd wait until the customers were served before heading out. He looked so handsome and adventurous in his special jeans with the extra padding on the front of the legs to protect him from the thorn-apple trees. Jack had a collection of Ernest Hemingway's writing and we had talked about visiting this writer's retreat in Cuba some day. At moments like this, I felt that I was married to my own Hemingway. Jack would have to walk through the store on his way to the backyard to get to his truck and my heart pumped a little faster at the sight of him in his hunting clothes. As he paused to kiss my forehead, the question was always the same: "Are you going to be all right alone?" "Sure," was my inevitable reply. And the coy look on his face when he would return with a bird or two and a lively discussion over supper was worth the small extra effort if the store had been very busy for the final two hours of the day.

I missed a lot of that sharing when Jack moved to the farm. He wasn't much of a telephone talker, so unless it was a holiday or a day off from the store for me, I never did get to hear of the grouse adventures after that.

Jack's ruffed grouse hunting allowed me to play 'gourmet' chef once in awhile. I did become a bit of an expert at cooking his partridge. If we had a couple of friends over for dinner and served his latest trophies, I could show off a little. By wrapping the breasts in tin foil, with a little margarine inside and a quarter of an apple, then roasting the tightly wrapped bird in a shallow baking pan, partly filled with water, at 325 degrees for an hour and twenty minutes, I provided our guests with a delicacy that was always enjoyed. In fact, many friends who did not eat food from the wild, made an exception for one of our gourmet partridge meals because the bird was moist and had a sweet chicken-like flavor that was delicious.

Jack became a good shot with his twenty-gauge shotgun, missing very few birds, even on the fly. I nicknamed him "hawk eye" because his eye was keen, and his hand steady, so he wasted very few shells. And he was a conservation-minded hunter who wouldn't bother to shoot if he didn't think he had a chance of finding the bird, or getting our spaniel out to look for it. Years ago, his best season was fifty-one birds, but in the past few years the birds had become less plentiful and a dozen birds in a season was normal fare. At one breast per person, that meant we could entertain only a couple of times to share our bounty, but those guests were carefully chosen and always appreciated the grouse feast.

For our thirty-fifth wedding anniversary, we decided that he would purchase a new twenty-guage shotgun, specially made in Italy. The Fair Company made a lightweight gun that Jack said would be handy as he was now in his sixtieth year, and after an afternoon of walking in the bush, it was very comfortable to be carrying a lighter load.

This purchase gave us the bonus of two more friends, Brian and Catherine Dwyre, who operate a gun shop north of Brockville. Their dedicated style of service made the expensive price tag easier to handle, and they even wished us belated anniversary wishes six months later when we went to pick up the imported gift.

The joy my husband received from that gift was worth every penny of the purchase price. He couldn't wait to get home to show it to his father-in-law and his son. He had to be convinced to spend the money on it because Jack was not the demanding type. Any money he ever needed for his hobbies had always come from a small allowance that he had taken each week from his pay. I looked after all the bill paying for our household needs, so Jack didn't have access to very much money. We believed in paying cash for most items we purchased, and lived within our means. His salary had never been as high as other graduates of the college in the same discipline. He used to joke with one of his friends who graduated with him that he made half of his friend's salary.

Fortunately for us, Jack and I never measured success or happiness in life by the size of his paycheck. What we did with the money was more important. We believed in tithing to our church, which resulted in our never being without, even during the lean years when one company he worked for downsized and he found himself out of a job after seven years. He worked for the city with a pick and shovel that summer to keep food on the table, and applied for every job he could.

I was making the equivalent of our grocery money, teaching baton twirling, and probably should have been working at some other job to help out. Jack did not expect it from me, and our children benefited by my being around when they needed me. Later, when I spent fifteen years managing our stationery business, I made up for my earlier part-time work commitment. In The Sanctuary, I dedicated six days a week, about nine hours a day, to operating the business. Looking back on this time, I am convinced that my service to my husband and our family business rewarded me tenfold by the closer relationship Jack and I had during this time. I wouldn't have missed this for all the money in the world.

When you buy a house that has no running water, you learn to do a lot of water carrying. Our house had a ten-foot dug well that seemed to be adequate, and the old hand pump still worked if you primed it properly. It took me a few tries to get the hang of the well pumping. The water was tested and found to contain traces of E. coli, so it was only good for washing floors and mixing cement, washing paint-brushes or feeding to the dog.

My little blue plastic washbasin was fine for the dishes, but it could handle only a couple of plates and one mug at a time. When company came for dinner (we decided early on in the renovation process that we would entertain friends despite the clutter of a half-finished house), we didn't expect company to help with dishes. The process of boiling the water and mixing in some cold water took forty minutes for a dinner for four. Besides, Jack never failed to pick up the towel and dry the dishes after dinner, which provided us with another time of sharing.

On one weekend visit early on in our habitation of the house, I remember looking at the white basin that we saved for washing our hands and taking little sponge baths. It was about a quarter full of light grey water, and I thought irritably that Jack must have forgotten to toss it out.

Only after I began living full-time at the farm did I understand that you do not throw out the water from the basin each time your hands need rinsing. Water is a precious commodity that is heavy when carried, so you wash your hands a few times in the same water, adding a little extra clean water to the basin whenever you need to rinse off your hands. There was no excuse for my critical heart when I spotted that partly filled basin with the not-so-perfect water, and it took a few months of living this lifestyle for me to fully appreciate the economical necessities of bush living.

We should be careful not to find fault with the small details in life. They are not as important as trusting that our spouse doesn't usually do things to frustrate us on purpose, and there is often a simple explanation for everything that happens.

With no plumbing in the house, Jack had no worries about pipes freezing in the winter. The toilets never overflowed, I had no bathrooms to clean on the weekends, or kitchen sinks to scrub. I tried to keep the outhouse painted each summer and even hung a few plaques on the wall. I had to substitute kitty litter for lye to keep the outhouse fresh because I found that my local hardware store no longer sold lye. Of course, a can of scented spray is a useful modern invention, as are the little "wet nappies" that are individually wrapped and very handy to leave in the outhouse.

One important early discovery we made was that the use of a cushioned toilet seat in an outhouse provides added comfort on February days. The cushioned seat does not retain the cold like a plastic seat. When it needs replacing, which will probably be quite soon as the screws have lost their ability to hold tight, I know I'll splurge and get another cushioned model.

A necessity in my life as a female pioneer in her mid-life years was my potty. A four-litre white plastic mayonnaise pail, complete with cover and carrying handle, had become my night commode, and was also especially helpful on cold or rainy days. The walk to the outhouse was not long but slightly miserable when the rain was pouring outside.

At the farm, I have used more bleach than I ever used in my whole married life, as it proved to be the perfect daily dose to keep the buckets 'hygienically correct.' I even picked up a second bucket for a guest potty, and my female friends are pleased with this bonus for middle-of-the-night use. I joked with our last sleepover guest that her room had an ensuite bathroom, in a manner of speaking. Men have always had a much easier time with such matters, and freedom of choice as to which tree to stand behind.

So country living, pioneer style, requires a versatile collection of buckets: the bucket for the mop, the slop bucket, the night bucket, the collection-of-rainwater bucket, the ash bucket, to mention only a few. Our son and daughter-in-law presented us with a large rain barrel that had its own tap, so we placed it near the outhouse and we were able to wash our hands in the spring, summer and fall with the water collected from the rain. I could also wash my paintbrushes from my studio. It felt luxurious to have this tap to use. I am sure Hattie would have welcomed such an invention in her day. There was a dry sink in the dining area, a non-functional hand pump in the summer kitchen, and an old cistern in the room over the summer kitchen, but they had probably only been in use several decades earlier when Hattie's parents were still alive and occupying the house.

Extra household chores are a big part of pioneer living, especially in the winter. Having a woodstove as the main source of heat means chopping wood regularly to keep up with the many cords required for our lengthy Canadian winters.

The first winter that Jack lived at the farm was a nightmare for him because his heat source was a small airtight woodstove that we had acquired several years before and had used in the basement of our first house. The stovepipes came upstairs and into the bedroom, which kept him warm enough at night, but he had to get up and feed the stove about every two hours. He often slept fully dressed, which simplified his trips downstairs to keep the fire going.

His second winter, we had made the three thousand dollar investment of a new woodstove that took a train ride all the way from British Columbia to our dealer, and then to our house. The "King" of stoves, a large airtight stove with a catalytic converter, worked well except that a stainless steel liner Jack had placed inside the original brick chimney was not the best solution for the smoke, and we wound up with a liquid creosote drip that had to be caught in a small bucket under the stovepipe. This pipe traveled through my "upper room" and the stench was not pleasant.

So the third winter, Jack decided we would make another investment and purchase a good-quality stainless-steel chimney that would receive the smoke directly from the stove and go up through the roof of the drive shed. This Selkirk-style chimney proved to be the right solution and solved the creosote problem. It was also handy for cleaning purposes.

The King needed to be fed at least four times a day, in the morning, the late afternoon, after supper, and the last feeding at about eleven at night. Since we were early risers, and got up to seven or eight hours of burn time out of the stove, the morning coals were usually still adequate to revive the fire in about fifteen minutes. The heat from the propane fireplace in the hallway near the stairs was a good supplement on very cold days, and helped to keep the upstairs bedrooms relatively warm.

When the temperature dipped below minus 20 degrees Celsius, you worked there or caught up on your reading in the library, or headed off to a neighbor's for a nice long visit.

Winter was a bit of a struggle, but that only enhanced the anticipation of spring. Jack was more frugal than he should have been about using the propane fireplace. With his long underwear and down-filled vest, and so much inside work to do, he used the propane fireplace only on weekends when I was visiting. There were a couple of very cold weeks when he told me that he had spent some extra time under the covers.

~

Garbage can be a problem in the country. Jack burned most of the paper and cardboard containers outside. That way, our two-garbage-bag limit was never surpassed. Burning refuse was another chore that needed to be done on selective days when the wind was not strong, it was not raining, and there was nothing else pressing to be done, because a burn barrel should be attended to at all times.

Jack's style was safety first and that was good protection. Especially when no insurance company would insure our house until it was completely finished. Perhaps this policy was new since the tragedy of September 11, 2001, but we tried many companies to get some coverage, and no one was interested. We realized that a fire in the country had very little chance of being controlled and was usually a complete loss. We asked for God to insure us until the house was complete, and knew He was expecting us to do our part by being very careful. We always double-checked the propane cooking range and the woodstove whenever we had to leave for a few hours. Once the plumbing and the wiring would be completed, and of course, the water running in the taps, then, an insurance broker advised me, we could apply for some insurance, which was estimated to be in the 'higher' price range.

Storage of extra canned goods was also an important task for the modern pioneer because the nearest store was miles away. Storage of such foodstuffs as rice and grains was handled by moving a large two-door metal filing cabinet from the store to use as a pantry. Totally mouse-proofed, it served as a kitchen necessity in an old house where mice are always visiting without an invitation.

In winter, a snowstorm can hit anytime, and despite a four-wheel-drive vehicle, it is best to have ample food on hand, just to be sure. Besides, there is no point in trying to get out before the plow if there is no emergency. Our township does an adequate job of clearing the roads once the snow has subsided. We have been snowed in only one Sunday morning when the snowplow was delayed by the storm, so when we did get out, we had to drive a little further to catch a later Sunday mass.

There are so many outside chores required by this style of life. A good riding lawn tractor is a necessity in order to cut the large grassy area. We limited our formal lawn space, and most of the front yard is wildflowers, lilac and apple trees, but it still takes two hours to cut the grass, and another hour for the trim with the weed eater. The grass is mostly the kind that city folks spray away from their perfect specimens of lawn. We have creeping charlie and crabgrass, mixed in with a modest amount of real grass. There is no next-door neighbor who might complain that our yard is not respectable enough for the street. Besides, it has come a long way from the first day we walked the property and had twelve- to twenty-inch-high brush to struggle through to get to the back door. The burdocks are the biggest nuisance and need to be dug out quickly in the spring, or they just reproduce themselves and provide a problem for the dog. He often spends an hour pulling out the burrs after a romp through the field.

I am not a flower gardener. I love to admire other people's gardens but have no patience for weeding or planting. We started a small perennial garden thanks to our daughter-in-law. Her mother is an avid gardener and donated several of her perennials for Sarah to plant for us. So I made a sign that says

"Sarah's Garden," and I have been trying to keep it weeded. I am not as successful as I should be and must work harder at that facet of my life next year. I love to watch the flowers appear, and take delight in the realization that they return each spring. I see all these as miracles and share this joy with Sarah.

Sarah began the garden for us before her marriage; now with her own magnificent garden to look after, she has less time for her little garden at the farm. Hopefully, *her* daughter will follow in the footsteps of her mother and Sarah's mother, Irene, and will love to plant things. Perhaps when she is old enough, Arianna will take care of this little garden for her Nanny who paints flowers far better than she gardens them.

There is an old machine shed on the property that had almost totally collapsed when we bought the farm. For several years it sat there looking as though the next big wind might push it down.

The odd thing was that a couple of rock elms seemed to be keeping the worst side from caving in completely. On a few occasions, friends suggested to Jack that he might want to tear it down. Another friend offered to get a crew together to rebuild it. Jack always thanked people for their suggestions but never seemed interested in a team effort to either tear this shed down or rebuild it. The last summer before I moved to the farm, Jack started work on this shed. He didn't talk about the project. He just tackled it.

The first week he opened it up, taking two sides of the wooden wallboards down and stacking them. John came out and helped his father take out some of the larger beams, and store them for later. Then the next week I noticed he had placed a come-a-long around one of the trees that was holding up the bad side and had attached it to the good wall beam opposite. It is not easy to explain the contraption he created. All I know is that in one week he had pulled the building back up a total of thirty-three inches. He would stretch the series of come–a-longs and place a small one-inch board at the bottom. He continued to do this, all the while making the building straighter. Quietly, with more determination than I had ever seen in him, he began to put the main corner beam straight and then laid a cement pad under it. He repeated this effort several more times in the front, and once the building was secure and straightened, he put a new crossbeam on the front. He then rebuilt the board and batten on the outside, recycling all of the old wood. It took Jack about three months to finish this project.

The year before, in the fall of 2002, we made the decision that since no one had come to buy our business, it was time to close the store. We had found a tenant to rent both the apartment and the empty store. The rents helped cover some of the major expenses of owning property downtown, such as property taxes, heat and power. We were without any extra renovation funding, so not much else could be done at that time.

It seemed providential that just about the time

Jack was thinking about starting the machine shed project we found a buyer for our building. Jack knew we were going to need extra storage for the things we would be moving from the store at the end of the year, and although he really didn't tell me, I sensed that the pending sale was the inspiration he needed to put the shed back to a useful condition. He also changed the windows of the shed, placing new second-hand windows on the second level. He made a new set of doors for it, that opened wide enough for John's Land Cruiser and our old International tractor.

That fall when some friends came out to visit who hadn't known about this project, Jack very proudly told them he had repaired it the old-fashioned way, one beam at a time. There was such joy in the little smile that came over his face when he sat sipping a beer that Sunday afternoon, knowing that the machine shed had been restored to working order. He had also tackled it early enough that it didn't interfere with the grouse-hunting season.

Dance of the Thunderbirds

Emily Carr had an eagle painted on the ceiling of her "House of All Sorts." Our farm had turkey vultures that came and soared on Sunday afternoons when we'd sit and sip a beer and relax from our week of working. It was such an entertaining performance as they caught the breezes, played in the sky above the old double barn, then landed on the metal roof to rest awhile and warm themselves in the summer sun.

I find the name turkey vulture has ugly connotations, so I nicknamed them my 'thunderbirds.' Their outline as they flew reminded me of the native art image I have seen so often. I had given them names on occasion. I called one of them

Wallace, after the Canadian poet Wallace Havelock Robb. Assuming that the two of them are mates, I called another Edna, after Mr. Robb's wife. I felt privileged to watch them soar and it seemed as though they waited for us to come outside to do their little dance in the sky. Perhaps they were proud of their ability to fly like eagles, and enjoyed the opportunity of sharing their gift with us. Watching their majestic flight, you don't see their small red heads. I would agree that the small head on such a large bird seems out of place, but it is easy to ignore this reality after seeing them soar.

The first time we saw them, there seemed to be only three birds. The next spring a couple more appeared, and the most recent count was eleven at one time.

When Langis, a birdwatcher from Ottawa, appeared on our doorstep doing research for a new breeding bird atlas, we told him of our vultures, and he requested a visit to our barn. He returned ten days later and discovered that our vultures had been nesting, and two white balls of fluff were shown to us, high up in the haymow of the old barn. We were warned not to approach too closely, as any human scent could frighten the baby birds. The discovery of this nesting was duly recorded. No doubt the turkey vultures found our abandoned barn a quiet place to raise their offspring.

With so many different species of birds surrounding us, there always seemed to be some activity. When the Baltimore orioles built a nest in an overhanging limb in front of the sunroom, we enjoyed their efforts at creating the woven masterpiece that became home to a couple of offspring. Keeping watch, we were also given a front-row seat to the flying lessons, once the babies had grown and were ready to leave the nest.

Last summer there was a bird rescue. A rose-breasted grosbeak flew against the window of the drive shed and knocked itself out. This colorful male seemed to be a goner, but Jack had observed the fall, so he picked up the bird and brought him to the picnic table. The bird lay very still and after about a half-hour rose to his feet. I am certain he was not enjoying the attention we were giving him, and we were not sure if he had broken a wing and would be able to fly. I started praying to St. Francis of Assisi, that famous animal and bird-loving saint. About two hours went by and the grosbeak just stood on the table, not moving. Finally, he attempted movement and hopped down to the ground. I think he was testing himself, checking his strength. Jack picked him up again and put him back on the table. About an hour later, having mustered all of his courage, and I am sure being helped by our belief in his ability to survive, the bird flew to a nearby apple tree. It was a moment worthy of celebration, and another bit of drama for our Sunday afternoon at the farm.

One of the annoying sounds that Jack was often tired of hearing in the spring was the phoebe's constant cry of "phee-bee, phee-bee," especially early in the morning before Jack's usual time to get up. But this bird loved to build a nest near our bedroom window, so we just had to accept this as our personal wake-up call.

One of the rare sightings we had was of the indigo bunting. The old apple tree south of the house seemed to attract this bird and we were treated to a visit once or twice. It never stayed around. There were plenty of sparrows of varying kinds, a cardinal or two, northern flickers, and downy and pileated woodpeckers who enjoyed our old trees. There was evidence that the north wall of the drive shed must have been of interest to the woodpeckers at one time because they had left their markings behind.

In the field beside the house, Jack pointed out the flight of a harrier that liked to check our grass for lunches. Also, I became quite expert at spotting the red-tailed hawks that passed by, and the green herons that dotted the early evening sky. He taught me to recognize the catbird, the killdeer plover and the nut-hatch, and my bird-spotting lessons resulted in a better enjoyment of our regular visitors. I am still not familiar with their songs or their calls, but that is something for future study.

I was cleaning out a box of odds and ends that Jack had kept in the garage of our first house. He had tossed these items in loosely with some old tools that he had packed up quickly over fifteen years before. I had given him a small wooden veneer wall plaque after one of our misunderstandings and he had kept it hanging in his office inside the garage. It read "I like you because I like me when I am with you." Finding this plaque again reminded me of some of the differences in our personalities, but I read the words with a new smile on my face because I had grown so much since then, and the words were even more meaningful to me now.

I also found a birthday card I sent to Jack in 1984. The message indicated a strong turning point in my relationship with him and also a growing of my faith in God:

I never knew what real love was until I learned from you. Real love is patient, forgiving, and understanding. It allows for growth and discovery. Real love is from God. You were sent to me from a loving

Father in Heaven. Thank God for you. May you have a great 42nd year!

Marriage is all about communication and it takes many years to learn how to communicate with your mate. No doubt this is the main challenge in marriage if we would only realize it. It is a roller-coaster ride full of ups and downs and much adventure. The secret is to persevere. That is the word I use often on the cards I send to young couples who invite me to their weddings. Never give up and never stop trying, I tell them. If we knew that there would be no one else for us to love and that we had to learn to get along with this person in our lives or we would forever be alone, I think that we would try harder. There are exceptions to this when the bond of matrimony is more of a show than a reality. Immaturity can be a drawback to any relationship and prevent a positive solution to the daily struggle of living together.

For a couple that goes to church on a regular basis, there is a bonus because God does arrange for us to be uplifted at Sunday services. I know that many a scripture hit home in my heart especially in the early years when my stubborn nature and selfish immaturity collided with my young husband's inexperience at relationships.

I took the crib apart and the children's clothes were packed one afternoon in our seventh year, and my wise father suggested to us that we talk over our problems one more time. We did, and things improved. At about seventeen years of marriage, I was complaining about my difficult husband to a new friend who happened to be a priest. This priest didn't mind telling me the truth about life. I told him how my reserved and quiet husband just didn't seem to understand my needs, and I never knew whether he was truly happy in our relationship. The old priest smiled and shook his head at me, and inquired, "Do you pray for your husband?" Of course I prayed. I asked God to make him into the kind of man who would make me happy.

"But do you pray for his needs…for his happiness …for him to be the best that he can be?" I had not looked at it that way. It was all about me, and what I thought I needed. It was a valuable lesson, and although it took several more years of effort, I finally discovered that the more I prayed for Jack's happiness and success in his own person, the more our relationship took on a more positive atmosphere. Praying for him allowed me to give God more control of our married life. I let go, becoming more peaceful from the act of praying for him, and he grew more confident about our marriage as the result of my prayers. It was a win-win situation.

Prayers do change people, and usually the change begins within your self first. The more we pray for others the more we benefit from the results. That same priest, Andre Peter Steinmann, an Oblate from Cap de La Madeleine, celebrated our twentieth anniversary mass for us, which proved to be a highlight in our marriage.

Just before our second Christmas at the farm, I mailed Jack a card. I often wrote to him, especially the first two years of our living separately. It was a good way to share my love for him, and since

I love writing letters anyway, who better than your spouse to send off a small gift of your love. That particular card said:

Dearest Grouse Champ and Golden Oaks Squire! I believe in Santa—I believe in love—I am in love with my "Santa" at Golden Oaks. I hope that you never get sick of 'Magnificat' bread, our Casa Maria brown, because I love the smell—I love the feel of the dough—and the joy of sharing the bread with others.

Miss you!

Love, J.L.E.

I didn't get return mail from Jack, but it was always nice to walk into the kitchen on Saturday night and see a card that I had sent that week sitting open on the window ledge. He collected dozens of them over the three years that we lived apart, and I know that the few minutes I took from my workday at the store gave him a boost when he picked up the mail at our box in Maxville. The pleasure of a card or a love letter can be read over and over again. Those stamps were a good investment and planted seeds of affirmation that blossomed into a closer bond of intimacy.

The old iron bed that came with the house must have belonged to Fred and Emily, Hattie's parents. The mattress was tired, but the springs were solid. In 1999, we acquired a second-hand mattress from our friend Gordon, and after scrubbing the frame, we made up our first double bed for sleeping in our new, old home.

In the beginning, we had placed the bed in the room that would become our library. The demolition had already been started in that room, so there was light coming from three windows. Of course, the tall trees kept the direct sunlight from coming through during the summer months, but this became the brightest area in the house. The size of the iron bed was much bigger than the trailer sleeping area had been, so our nights were far more comfortable, and far less claustrophobic.

It was truly a special event when I arrived at the farm about six months after Jack had moved there and discovered that our old iron bed was now in its proper place and the bedroom had been drywalled and painted blue. He had changed the door to our bedroom, closing the original door frame and creating a closet there, and transferring this frame to a north wall to make the new entrance. He always amazed me with these ideas that he had. Our bedroom now opened into the library, and the light from one of the library windows helped to light our bedroom.

I loved lying in bed at night and looking out the window at the shadows of the tree branches. In winter they seemed to stand watch over the back of the house. In spring, their blooming looked just as exciting at night as in the daytime because the outline of the branches was constantly changing. In summer, we would go to bed before it was completely dark, and I had the pleasure of seeing the fullness of the branches, laden with their leaves, and of course, the joy of each new spring and summer morning when those branches became the performance platforms for the song of the birds. Autumn held its own magic because each day the branches lost a few more leaves, sometimes quickly, during a strong breeze, or very slowly, one leaf at a time falling to the earth, like a farewell dance as it swayed and gently made its final exit. When the full moon appeared each month in the night sky, the moon shadows danced and played their romantic pirouettes along the ground below my window.

One starry spring night, Jack and I set up the telescope outside to get a good look at Mars. The beauty of the many constellations was breathtaking and truly made us feel like millionaires. Only the howl of the coyotes far off in the distance made me shudder after I had crawled into our old iron bed. Of course, all I had to do was reach my hand across the bed and touch Jack's back, and I felt safe again. Married love expressed through moments of intimacy is the closest thing to heaven that I have so far imagined.

It wasn't so much the passion between us,

especially after over thirty years of sleeping in a double bed together. It was the pleasure of pleasing one another. That seems to me to be the ultimate goal in the physical portion of married love experience: wanting to bring joy and peace to the heart and soul of your mate through gentle and sincere caresses of their body. The time it takes should never matter. In a few minutes of loving touches, you can feel as though the cares of the world have all disappeared.

I remember the first weekend I visited Jack in the spring after he had moved permanently to the farm. He had not been particularly talkative that day, but I had been busying myself with cleaning out old letters and files, and getting rid of some of the excesses of my life. There was a particular file of letters from my past that I wanted to dispose of, and so I asked him if he would be putting on a fire in the burn can that day. He said that he would, so I took this file of letters and diary pages and put them into the flames of the outside barrel that he used to burn paper refuse.

The file contained negative diary pages, now about twenty years old, comparing first love to my married state. The words had been written during a time of uncertainty that happens often in the early years of marriage. One sometimes has difficulty adjusting and learning how to live within the confines of married life. Of course, by the grace of God and perseverance, life goes on, and if we are lucky, our spouse is patient with these growing-up years, and the marriage survives. I knew that these pages of 'heart pouring' and pining for the yesterdays that had long ago disappeared were of no significance now. They represented a time when I had been learning to let go of the disappointments of the past, accept the present, and find hope in the future. Jack had no idea what was being burned in that file folder, but I discovered that God knew what was in my heart and so He gave me a special reward at the end of that day.

When Jack and I got ready for bed, early because we were both tired and it was an especially hot evening, even for May, we both stripped down to a T-shirt and underwear, and lay side by side in silence. His hand found mine, he gripped it tightly, and as if he had received an inspiration from my yearning heart, Jack asked me, "How would you like to play for awhile?" What he meant was that we would spend some time just caressing one another and sharing that special kind of intimacy we had not enjoyed or truly expressed since we were first in love, and stealing passionate moments in my art studio before we were married.

Nothing could have pleased me more than to hear these words from him, and the cherished reality is that this was not an isolated evening in May. For almost every weekend, except when one of us was ill, or too tired to stay awake, we shared an intimate and playful visit in the old iron bed. Sometimes it was at three o'clock on a Sunday morning, and I would crawl out of bed an hour later to make my weekly batch of whole-wheat bread. Sometimes it would only be an affectionate fifteen minutes on a Monday morning, just before we had to quickly dress and head back to town to open our business for another week. The point is that it became an important part of our new life at the farm, and seemed to be something that Jack might have been anticipating all week. I guess he must have seen me in a new light; perhaps I became his weekend girlfriend, or his Saturday night date. For whatever the reason, our relationship quietly took on an intimate, more affectionate depth. There was a new closeness that I had always hoped would happen, but had not recently experienced.

We never discussed this new change in our relationship. It always seemed more mysterious and romantic to Jack not to talk about these things after the fact, or especially, beforehand. The hunter in him liked to surprise me in the middle of the night by reaching over to see if I was awake, and then holding me. I knew that was his signal that if I was awake, then it was 'playtime' and I welcomed these moments with all of my heart.

Unlike youthful desires that demand self-gratification or a "what about me?" search for physical satisfaction, our moments of intimacy had almost taken on an out-of-this-world atmosphere. There were times that I felt so satisfied from his caresses that I thought my soul would explode. It seemed like a taste of heaven to see his smile of satisfaction and to know that I had given him such pleasure. He felt the same, I am sure, because he never complained or demanded more than I could give to him. It was genuine affection that comes from being committed and trusting that your spouse wants only the best for you. That kind of trust can often take many years to develop, and I was so fortunate that I had received the ultimate in love from my husband. I so often said a prayer of thanksgiving after Jack had fallen asleep, because I was bursting with the joy of having someone so wonderful beside me to love. And there were times when I felt I could never be any happier than I was at that moment. Only God alone knew the peace and happiness that was filling my heart to have discovered this special man.

I believe that couples should never forget that as long as they are struggling to do better, and seek reconciliation when needed, they can travel a road that knows no limitations of love. As we profess our wedding vows before God, He will grant us a sacrament that is a living entity that can continue to grow stronger and become a powerful tool, especially in the later years of our marriage. I learned just how powerful it can be when we turn our troubles in our married life over to God and let Him fix them, without our interference. We all need to learn to receive, to accept, and to praise our partner; to be thankful, to pray, and to forgive. Every day is a new beginning, and resentment has no place in a good marriage.

I cried a lot of tears for our first twenty years, but looking back I realize that it was mostly when I didn't get my own way, or when I spoke too soon and didn't give my husband a chance to express his viewpoint. Christ tells us that we should treat each other as though we are dealing with Him directly. I didn't always do that. Thank God I learned how to be submissive to God's will for my marriage before it was too late.

Without power or lights to turn on, our bedroom was often flooded by the light of the moon. We watched many a moonrise, and when it was full, you hardly needed a flashlight to find your way down the stairs in the middle of the night. What an incredible delight to watch the moon shadows playing outside on the winter snow, or lighting up the backyard full of autumn leaves.

From Jack I learned about the equinox and the solstice. I had heard those words but never understood them until Jack began living at the farm full-time. I saw the pleasures of the changing light in the mornings in January. It may only happen a few minutes at a time, but as we grow older, days quickly turn into weeks, and weeks into months, so the longer hours of daylight impact with more significance. I often got up before the sun on the weekends and had the pleasure of those twilights that Jack taught me to appreciate.

Sunday mornings had been extra special since we bought the farm because our morning routine included a visit to our local antique shop, which occupied a white wooden building, the former Presbyterian church in the village of Monkland. This church was located just a couple of doors down the road from St. Michael's, the Roman Catholic chapel, where our service would finish some fifteen minutes before ten in the morning. The standard opening time on the other church door stated ten o'clock, but quite often, once Richard, the proprietor, became our friend, he made a point of getting to his church ahead of time, and welcoming us as his first customers of the day. We teased him that our visit to his shop was our "church after church." We were able to sell him some of our old antique toys, pencils, pens and metal clickers that we had accumulated over the years, and in turn we were able to pick up a couple of trunks, dressers and even an old sideboard, which we got for a very good price because there was a streak of acrylic paint across its top. (A white lace cloth is hiding that defect until time permits me to strip it and give it a facelift.)

I would bring extra cash with me some of the time, and Rick always felt that our visit started his day well. Even when we might only spend ten or twenty dollars, he would let us know the following Sunday that we had been a catalyst to his having had a very good day. Whether we really were his good luck charms or not, Rick was the type of person who made his customers feel good about visiting his shop. He always wore a smile and enjoyed the encounter, whether money changed hands or not.

Once in awhile, after we had become Sunday-morning regulars, I would find a particular trinket, and then our friendly shop owner would say, "Take it home. It's free today." But I would always leave a dollar or two on his counter in exchange for my treasure. I wanted my purchase to give him his beginning of cash flow for the day. We felt our own day was brightened by a visit to the "church after church."

Jack's favorite shopping was done in the back of the building, where the rusted unsellables were kept. He would go out snooping in the back and check for a part he might be needing, or a barrel that might be poking through the pile of interesting odds and ends that our friend had picked up as extras when visiting a house sale or an auction. When Jack found a particular item that had been out in the back for several months, Rick would usually say, "Now, that is really a good deal today. Take it home. You are doing me a favor. Somebody will only steal it," or he might comment, "You take it before the rain destroys what's left of it." And Jack would smile that special smile that finding a bargain gives, and occasionally, he would bring Rick something from his old barn the next week, to add to the pile for the next person who liked to go through the interesting items behind the church building. We both found it so satisfying to deal with someone who valued customer satisfaction above the almighty dollar. These business people are rare indeed.

Rick and Lorraine had also been a great source of drinking water fill-ups and occasional showers. They never minded a call to inquire if a visit for a shower was permitted. Rick once kidded Jack that the price of a shower was a quarter, which was much less expensive than the days of the Old West when a Saturday night bath could cost a cowboy a whole dollar. They also were frequent dinner guests and helped us celebrate St. Patrick's Day, the First of July, and of course, they were regulars at our Christmas gathering.

It was October 22, 2000, a perfect fall day, just a few months after Jack was living at the farm full-time. There was stillness in the air that Sunday afternoon. Some friends had stopped to visit on this sunny day to share the beauty of the autumn colors and were just about to leave when we noticed a lot of activity at the Dewar farm next door. I thought I saw a fire truck there, and then a little black car came up our driveway. The young man behind the wheel asked if there was a 'Joan' around. I answered that I was Joan and he said, "Come with me. Jean needs you. She just found Jim and he's dead."

I left Jack and went up the road with the young man. I consoled my friend Jean until her daughters arrived. Her husband, Jim, had fallen from the platform of the corn wagon and he had become tangled in the corn auger. When he hadn't come in for his lunch, Jean had become worried. He was dead when she found him.

Those next few weeks following Jim's funeral were very difficult for Jack because he and Jim had known each other long before we bought the farm. He would no longer be able to see him drive down the road on his tractor, or just have him stop by for the odd beer.

Jim and Jean had been our first dinner guests, sharing a pre-cooked chicken and a bottle of wine in our unfinished house. The welcome that Jean had given me the first time I visited her for tea was an encouraging sign to me that my future life at Hattie's farm would be special. It was wonderful to be able to walk up the road to her house to visit on a Sunday afternoon, to get away from the dust and the noise of the old lathe and plaster walls being removed. Jean and I had been looking forward to being full-time neighbors, but about a year and a half following Jim's death, she sold her farm and moved to the city.

Real retirement came to us the summer of 2003, when we finally sold our downtown building. It happened quite miraculously, or as those who do not put all of their lives into God's hands may call it, serendipitously. I liked giving God credit for every success that came our way.

The phone call came on July 16. We had listed the property with Joe, the same agent who had sold us the business and the building seventeen years earlier. He had already made an attempt to sell the building and business as a combination deal three years earlier, but with no luck. People had said to try another agent and I was not really sure what to do.

I prayed for an answer when Joe called me that same week and asked if I was going to list the building. So I met with him and decided on a price, and my husband agreed that we were doing the right thing. I told Joe that I was asking St. Joseph for his intercession and that at least he had the right name. It only took two weeks for the offer to come in. There were a few snags, but the deal was finalized in August 2003, and the details suited us all.

Our tenant in the bookstore had agreed that he would vacate the premises if we found a buyer. It was such a blessing that the future owners were not anxious and asked for an end-of-the-year closing date. We informed the apartment tenants that for now they would not be required to move. So we all made our plans.

Jack began taking loads home to the farm every time he came to town, and I began sorting the old antiques for a pending auction. Tim, the book man who had leased the store that March, was content that it would be business as usual until the end of the year for his second-hand bookstore. I am sure that all the work he did to fix up the store helped to make the sale. I think it is always an advantage to sell a property when it is occupied rather than empty.

We were all very busy that fall and excited about the future. Tim was planning to return Down Under for his sixth visit, and so he began to make travel arrangements for another trip to Australia and New Zealand early in the New Year.

In November, Jack came into town and announced to Tim and I that we should plan a little gathering for New Year's Eve at the store. He thought it would give us all a chance to say goodbye to former customers and city friends, and also to the building. Tim agreed and so I made up an informal invitation, put it on festive red paper and sent it out to about fifty of our friends and Tim's friends. The ironic thing is that I had always been the party planner in our family, but all of a sudden it was Jack the loner, the solitary man, the bushman, who was making the suggestion and was so excited about this gathering.

We planned it for an early evening wine and cheese beginning at six o'clock on New Year's Eve. The store had been emptied out and extra chairs borrowed from Shelley and Frank, the upstairs tenants. The side counters provided us with a place to put out the refreshments. I had spent the afternoon upstairs in the apartment, making sandwiches and enjoying the chance to visit in my old living quarters.

We had great response and over forty people stopped by, shared their memories about our business and the former business that had occupied the building. Even my parents who hadn't been out on New Year's Eve for a couple of decades, decided that this was a special occasion and joined us for the celebration of the end of an era. Our doctor, our children, many long-time friends and business neighbors came to wish us well for the coming year. The party lasted only a couple of hours, but you could feel the love in the room.

The whole day was a sentimental journey. We received a few bottles of champagne and some other retirement gifts. When we turned out the lights that night and drove back to the farm, we felt very content and optimistic about the year that was soon to begin.

The party had been dubbed The Final Farewell, and it was an appropriate choice of names because it proved to be the last gathering for my husband Jack. He and I visited the lawyer's office and collected the check for the sale of the building on the second day of January. The family lawyer, Ted Castle, our son's father-in-law, was taking care of the legal matters for us, and he shared our joy as he shook hands with Jack and gave me a congratulatory hug, wishing us well in our retirement.

There was no one more shocked than he and his wife Irene to learn that Jack had died, just three days later, on the fifth of January. For most of the people who had attended the New Year's party, it really was their final visit with my husband. It seemed to be such a happy time with so many plans and so much future ahead of us. Those good wishes of loving friends kept me going the following week when I faced Jack's funeral. I can only look back now with peace in my heart that my husband died at the happiest time of his life. He had even held his beautiful granddaughter, Arianna, for the first time on Christmas day the week before.

That Monday, January 5, was the beginning of my first week living at the farm full-time. It was a nice bright winter day despite the forecast of a storm. After our trip to the Laundromat, Jack decided he'd go down the road to have a coffee with his friend Pete. I was busy taking apart the Christmas tree.

"I forgot to tie it to the hook on the stairs," he commented and then he smiled and added, "It must have been a perfect tree." He had noticed the empty hook did not have its usual string attached to the tree as he climbed the stairs to change his clothes. Jack had "visiting town" clothes and work clothes and never complained about having to dress up in his better jeans for his public appearances off the farm, and then get back into his work clothes upon returning home. Actually, Jack was not ever the complaining type. Over the years, he had scolded me several times for my whining and complaining. He taught me that complaints use our energy and can bring our partner into a negative mood. It was far better to remain quiet in a difficult situation and solve the problem, instead of complaining about things.

I seemed to be in a daze on this first Monday of the first week of a new year. I found myself flitting from thing to thing, wanting to do so many different things because I was finally home, anxious to begin my new life, officially retired and on my way to becoming a valid country girl.

After the Christmas tree had been dismantled, I

noticed Jack's sweater lying on the back of a dining room chair. For months I had wanted to sew the broken seam under the arm, and so I decided, it was now or never. I was sitting at the dining room table when Jack returned from his visit to the neighbor. He mumbled something from the kitchen, but I couldn't quite make it out. I saw him again about twenty minutes later, from the sunroom window, when I carried a large statue from my studio down to clear the corner where my new bookshelves would go. That was the only thing I really wanted for Christmas from Jack. He bought the shelves for me, but also surprised me with a blue lounging suit that I had worn on Christmas Day. I didn't feel much like dressing up, because I had a bad cold, and just wanted to be comfortable.

From the sunroom window, I could see that Jack was wearing his red coveralls and pushing the all-terrain vehicle that belonged to his friend. He had been storing it in the machine shed for him. I wanted to open the door and offer to help him push it, but then I also didn't want to intrude. He never liked help unless he asked for it. A few times in the weeks of packing and moving, he had asked me to lift one end of an item, but mostly he was independent and could manage to move almost anything all alone.

I assumed he was going for a ride on the ATV, and so I carried on for the next few hours, moving things, taking boxes upstairs, and stopping long enough to pray my rosary, which I hadn't done that morning.

It began to get cool in the house, and I wondered for a moment why Jack had not returned to put another log in the woodstove. Keeping the house warm was his department. I had never even inquired as to how to use the stove, but was planning on learning about those details of our pioneer life after I had come home to stay.

As twilight began to settle, I looked out the window towards the road, thinking that Jack should be coming back soon. It was getting cooler, and he never forgot about his duties. I lit a candle and put it in the window, and stood for several minutes, gazing towards the road, wishing I could see him.

We can all let our imaginations run away from us when someone we are expecting is delayed, but I felt a stirring in my heart, an ache that something was wrong. My thoughts began to be filled with panic.

Nature called, and so the dog and I headed outside to the outhouse. To get there, you turn right at the door of the back shed. It was darker now, so when I returned to the house, I felt the urge to grab a flashlight and begin to look for Jack.

This time, I walked outside and turned to my left, and as soon as I rounded the corner of the drive shed, I saw our truck, parked towards the road, the trailer attached to the truck, and the ATV half-loaded on the trailer. I flashed the light towards the end of the trailer and I saw his green boots. I rushed over to him, and he was lying on his back. As I knelt down, I felt his face, which was very cold. He was looking towards the sky. His arms lay open on the ground as if he had accepted whatever fate had befallen him. I closed his eyes and prayed out loud for Jesus to bring him back to life. I held Jack's head in my hands for a moment or two, and then returned to the house to get a blanket. I called our friends Rick and Lorraine because I knew that Lorraine knew CPR. I went back outside to wait beside Jack, not wanting him to be alone. When they arrived, I returned to the house to call 9-1-1. I felt in my heart that Jack was gone, but my friend tried CPR for about fifteen minutes, while we waited for the ambulance to arrive.

Rick parked his truck on the road with his headlights on so that the ambulance could find us. Our farm is isolated, about three hundred yards from the nearest intersection, and without power it was hard to see the house. There was only the light from one propane lamp in the kitchen.

When the paramedics placed Jack on the stretcher and into the back of the ambulance, I felt disconnected from him. It was as if my heart knew that he was not coming back, and I had better begin to sever my ties with his physical presence. I also felt God's grace beginning to descend on my spirit, and after calling our son John, who would be meeting us at the hospital, I climbed into my friends' truck to make the trip to the hospital with them. I don't even remember whether I locked up the house. I had put the dog away in his cage, and I knew that the police officers were still on the scene. I really don't recall all of the details.

The emergency room staff of the small community hospital were very professional and the doctor on duty tried to warm up Jack's very cold body. He told me that they were going to try, but if they were able to bring him back, his brain would never return. When I heard this, I gave thanks to God that Jack had already died and would not be facing a future of hopelessness, his body alive without his mind.

We had called for Father Kelvin, a priest friend who lived near by, and he prayed over Jack, then offered my son and me the Blessed Sacrament and prayers to sustain us in this difficult time. He had known us thirty years, and we were grateful that he was at home that evening.

My son saw his father lying bare-chested, his face purple after the medical staff had tried to warm him up. I touched Jack's bare shoulder, making the sign of the cross on him, and walked away. I knew that the man I had loved for thirty-seven years was no longer there; only the shell of his body remained.

The coroner arrived, and we waited while he made his examination. He then gave us a thorough analysis of the situation, and his assumption at that point was that Jack had died from a sudden heart attack. His full report would follow in a few days, after the autopsy.

Lorraine and Rick offered to keep the fire going, care for the dog, and stay at the house for as long as we needed them. It was providence that they had cared for Jessie for three days the summer before, when Jack and I had traveled to visit his sister. They were used to the dog's routine, and he was very comfortable with them. There needed to be some wood splitting done to keep the woodstove going. Rick and Lorraine had recently retired from operating a dairy farm, and so wood stoves and country living were very familiar to them. The temperature had dropped that week to minus 27 degrees Celsius, and it ended up being the coldest week of the year.

At the hospital, the nurse handed us Jack's clothes and his boots. She put his chain with the scapular medal in my hand, and I held it tightly all the way home. This medal of protection had been on my husband's neck since I first met him. I gave it to our son John as I said good night to him later that evening.

I knew it would be best to spend the night in town with my parents, so I grabbed a change of clothes and traveled with John to town. We began to discuss the initial funeral arrangements together after we stopped to pick up my daughter on the way to my parents' apartment. Walking through the door of my parents' apartment was a very difficult part of that night. I stood before my parents, who are in their eighties, and said I had some bad news. My mother looked at me and saw that it must be terrible news, and since Jack had not walked in with us, she quickly assumed that it was him. I told her that he had died suddenly. How very much it hurt to have to speak those words to her. The pain in my heart showed on my face, and must have reminded her of the time that Jack had walked into the schoolyard where she was teaching to inform her that her son Eddy had had an accident and he was dead. My brother Eddy was only twenty-nine when he died. Jack was fortunate to have seen his sixty-first birthday.

The love that emanates from family members at a time like this is of great comfort. My sister Diana arrived two days later, to be of whatever help she could. My other sister, Carol Anne, joined us the next day, and they both hovered over me with the kind of caring I had never known before from them. Of course, I had never been a widow before. Jack's only sibling, Betty Ann, took the news very hard. Although they did not see each other more than once a year, Jack and Betty Ann were very close and often spoke on the telephone. She and her husband, Jim, made their travel plans immediately.

Lisa and John helped to arrange the funeral, picking the casket, choosing the flowers, and making the display of photos that would be shown at the funeral home for the wake.

When we approached the open casket for the first time at the funeral home on the day of visitation, we noticed that the expression on Jack's face seemed unusually calm. The funeral director had known Jack and I, as his establishment was a neighboring business, situated just a block from our former store building. Jack was a handsome man, and he now looked as if he was just having a peaceful sleep. There was no pain on his face from the struggle of a difficult passing but a slight smile instead.

The picture we had chosen for the newspaper was taken at John's wedding to Sarah, and Jack was wearing a tuxedo. When I saw it in the paper the next day, he looked like a movie star to me.

The large church where we had been married thirty-six years earlier was three-quarters full, and there were five priests and a deacon concelebrating the funeral mass. One of those priests, Monsignor Thomas Raby, had traveled from Napanee, some three hours away, to attend the funeral. He had been very close to Jack, and had renewed our vows in a private mass for our twenty-fifth anniversary. Our good friends Rudi and Cheryl, who had been with us on that special day, were away in Florida, and would not be able to share his funeral.

John's eulogy for his father was fitting and memorable. The pastor, Father Kevin, asked him to deliver his comments just prior to the mass beginning, and the congregation responded with spontaneous applause when he sat down.

John spoke about his father's interest in the outdoors, and his desire to purchase Hattie's farm. I had forgotten that John had hunted there with his dad many years before we bought it. John told everyone how he had given his father the nickname "Crazy Jack" when his dad decided to move to the farm permanently, and live without power, water and the other amenities we take for granted in the city. One of the most touching moments came when John commented:

For those of you who didn't know this, my father came from very humble beginnings. He tried to instill in his family the value of a dollar and how important it was to save your money, and not waste it on frivolous things. When I was a teenager I spent most of my money on music, guitars and girls. I was always showering my dates with gifts, which would drive my dad crazy. On many occasions he tried to get me to stop wasting all my money. He would say, "You need to invest your money in your future." I remember that on the day I married my wife, Sarah, Dad said to me with a coy smile, "I guess your investments have finally paid off."

I remember listening to the words of the funeral mass, and fingering the gold cross on my neck that had been a gift from Jack for our thirtieth wedding anniversary. We used to joke that I was dressing up in my "diamonds" whenever I put the necklace on. The cross had a very small diamond chip in the center of it, and it was the only diamond Jack had ever given to me. We were married so quickly that we had not bothered with an engagement ring, and besides, we only had enough money for two gold bands. When he surprised me with that little cross with the diamond in it, he was acknowledging not only his love for me, but his respect for our shared faith in God. There was no gift he could have given to me that would have made me any happier.

Gifts

We have all heard the expression, "God only gives you what you can handle and nothing more." I have learned another lesson these many months: that He also puts things into place so that you can handle the pain or the problems that life offers. He came quickly for Jack that cold January day, but He also made sure that I would be able to survive the new life that I was facing.

My friend Sally learned of Jack's death through the priest who anointed him at the hospital, and immediately called other 'friends of God' who began to pray for strength for my family and me. Jennifer came from Lancaster to stay with me every

Wednesday for several weeks, and there was such comfort in her visits. Sue had come to the funeral from Collingwood and arranged to remain a few extra days to keep me company at the farm. She had prior experience with our pioneer style of life, because the Christmas before, she had been our guest for a week. Many friends brought nourishing suppers and stayed to eat with me. Their visits gave me something to look forward to at the end of my day, and the meals they shared helped ease the pain in my heart.

The Bible says, "There is no greater gift than to lay down your life for your friends." Jack died while helping a friend. Well, the friend wasn't actually standing beside him, but Jack had been loading his friend's all-terrain vehicle that had been stored in our machine shed, onto his trailer. Jack was always willing to lend a hand when needed. This was an important part of his everyday life, especially since he had left the business world, and was enjoying country living. There might be a half mile between you and your nearest neighbor, but it was nice to know that you were there for each other.

About a week after Jack's passing, I phoned my nearest neighbor, Barbara, who lives about a quarter of a mile away. Although she had been living in the house up the road all the time that we had owned the farm, and for many years before, I had never met her. She came down to the house the next day for tea, and I inquired if I could have a ride to town with her once in awhile. She told me that she traveled to Cornwall at least twice a week, so for the next five months until John found a vehicle for me to purchase, I was a grateful passenger. It was interesting to learn more about the area from her, and to hear stories about Hattie, whom Barbara had known well. Hattie had brought little gifts for her daughters each birthday, and the Glen family had visited Hattie's house often.

I still made my whole-wheat bread every couple of weeks, so Barb was the recipient of one of the loaves in most every batch. Rick and Lorraine also gained a loaf of my bread each time I made it.

They continued to provide a place for me to shower, and picked me up if they were heading into town. I have never heard either of these neighbors hint that helping me was an effort. Sharyn and Gary, two other friends whose home was ten minutes in the other direction and who traveled to town every day, were very willing to drive out of their way to give me a lift. They were also frequent suppliers of supper and a shower.

Lisa phoned me every day and sent out little care packages of food. John came out every few days with supplies and to chop wood, and as soon as it became spring-like, he began a refresher course for me on driving. I had a valid license but had not used it for quite a few years.

My thoughtful daughter-in-law, Sarah, opened her heart even wider, allowing her husband to spend a lot of time at the farm helping his mother.

My parents welcomed me for showers and lunches, and helped with a listening ear when decisions had to be made. When I was trying to decide if I should stay at the farm or move to town, they even offered to move in with me.

That was perhaps the most difficult decision I had to make. Do I follow through with Jack's dream of finishing the house renovations, or do I sell the property as is and move back to the city I had left just a few weeks earlier. As an exercise, I began looking at houses. They say that a new widow should not move or make any major decisions regarding lifestyle for at least one full year, but my situation was very different. I was facing life in a house without power, running water or a toilet, and with a woodstove to manage in the winter. To top it off, I was not an experienced driver, so my situation warranted a look around at the housing market.

John and Sarah made several appointments for me, and each house that I could afford had many drawbacks. My country house had a large studio room, which would be a perfect place to paint. No house I saw with the real estate agent had equivalent space. Jack had refitted new windows on every window of our farmhouse. Most of the places I saw had old windows, some of them painted shut, and in need of replacing. My present home had new doors and a strong sub-floor, which had recently replaced the sagging floor in the original log portion of the house. Many of the houses I visited had crooked floors, only a half-storey upstairs and no closets. Granted, I was looking at older homes because they were within my price range. The trouble was that the market had suddenly become hotter because of the drop in interest rates, and single houses were scarce.

Finally after two weeks of serious searching, John presented me with a letter. It basically told me that he thought I should remain where I was, finish the project, and then decide in a year or so if I wanted to move. He also encouraged me by saying that he and Sarah would help with the renovations. It was a loving letter and confirmed my thinking that I was better off at "Jack's Farm" than in any of the dwellings I had looked at for possible purchase.

Then John and Sarah gifted me just a few weeks later with a beautiful hand-carved wooden sign that had been created especially for me. There was a sketch of a ruffed grouse decorating it, the type my husband loved to hunt, and it said: Jack's Farm, EST. 1996.

John says he feels that the farm is his legacy. It has helped him to mourn his father's passing by being able to complete many of the projects his father had started.

Surprised by God

By the grace of God, I have almost completed my first year of widowhood.

The biggest hurdle was learning to live without Jack's smile, without his voice, without the sharing of our daily routine. He knew me better than anyone else, and the things we shared were intimate realities of our life together that no one else would ever understand or want to share. Children are great comforters; they listen and they help all they can. But they cannot replace the bond that exists in a loving relationship with a spouse.

I couldn't sleep in our bed for the first month or so after Jack died. I felt safer sleeping instead in the smaller, adjacent bedroom. I had been sleeping in there the week before he died because Jack and I both had bad colds. I thought it easier not to disturb him with my coughing in the night so I chose to sleep apart from him. Over those days, he would get up about midnight to tend to the woodstove and stop by the little room at the top of the stairs. If he heard me stirring he would ask, "Are you okay?" I would tell him that I was fine and he would go back to our room. There was such comfort in those three words and I miss hearing them so much.

Just six months prior to my husband's passing, I spent a week helping a close friend go through the preparations of her husband's death and funeral. Abeba had called me early one Tuesday and simply said, "He's gone. Can you come?" I was in town that morning taking a shower at my parents' apartment. Although her husband had terminal cancer, we were thinking he still had another few weeks of life left. She, too, was surprised when she awoke that morning to see her husband lying there with one hand in relaxed fashion under his head, as if he had gently dozed off. He had slipped away quietly and peacefully in the night, while she was resting on a couch near his rented hospital bed. His wish was to die at home, and God permitted it. That morning as I passed the sign in my mother's apartment lobby, I saw these words: *Today speak words of compassion. You can help to soften the sorrow of a friend.* They were prophetic. Helping Abeba go through that week seemed to have been a dress rehearsal for my own bereavement that came about so soon after.

God sometimes gives you warning that a change is coming; with Jack's death, I got the surprise of my life. I had two choices. I had to accept His will or become angry, and I love the Lord too much to waste my energy that way. It still was difficult because tears have a way of coming upon you when you least expect them. In the early weeks, you might be busy doing your housework and all of a sudden the flood of emotion covers you and you have to stop and cry. There is no explanation for it except that your mind, heart and emotions are adjusting and tears are part of the grieving process. The miracle is that each time you cry, you are a taking a step forward in your healing.

I did not try to do a lot for the first few weeks of widowhood. My Springer spaniel, Jessie, enjoyed sitting with me on the couch in the sunroom while I was reading, and although he didn't understand when my tears burst forth, it was good to have him there beside me. When I finished crying, I would snuggle my head near him, pat him a few times, and tell him out loud (so I could hear myself affirming my situation) that, together, we would get through this painful time of adjustment.

I had purchased a new red hardcover journal to begin my new life with Jack at the farm in January 2004. The first entry was written January 13, and it definitely was not the diary entry that I had planned for it. I did a lot of writing as I began my walk through the tunnel of grief. My journal of remembrance proved to be excellent therapy.

The house in the woods made it easier for me to think clearly and face the reality of my new life. I enjoyed seeing a different scene from the window of the sunroom every day. I had many new things to learn, like how to put wood into a woodstove, and how to live a simpler life without the amenities of power and water. I had to learn to drive again, and to keep an eye on the propane supply and call for a refill. I had to shovel the pathway to the outhouse whenever it snowed, and eat alone. I even learned how to set the old-fashioned style of mousetraps, and my mouse count is almost at the first dozen. I had to learn to take care of myself because the man I depended on for so many practical things was no longer with me.

It is not easy, but I have come to realize that with my hand in God's hand I am stronger than I thought I was. And because I believe in eternal life, I feel confident that my husband is very much aware of my daily struggles and my needs, and he will instill in my spirit, the awareness of how to solve some of the daily problems that are unfamiliar to a city girl like me. I call out to him often, especially when I have difficulty or I am treading in unfamiliar water. He doesn't answer back, but it seems that very little time passes before the problem has a solution.

About a year before he died, Jack questioned me, asking if I would be happy living in the bush. He actually wondered aloud if maybe we should sell the property and move back to the city. Looking back, I think he might have been having a discouraging week and just needed confirmation that this whole crazy plan of pioneer living was still valid. My response was that his dream had become my dream and I couldn't wait to live with him, happily ever after.

When I stop to ponder the sequence of events that occurred just prior to Jack's death, my faith in God is strengthened. It would be so easy to feel sorry that we didn't have much time together here at the farm, but we did have so many great weekend visits. I remember joking just before Christmas that soon we might need another clothes closet. The closet in our bedroom was packed full with Jack's clothes and the big closet in my studio room had a lot of his hunting vests and outdoor clothing filling over half the space. I did not have a large wardrobe to move out, but we might have a tight squeeze until we had sorted and donated the things that we hadn't worn for a few years. When I was cleaning out the closets, preparing to give away some of Jack's clothes a few months later, I said: "Lord, You didn't have to take my roommate away to make extra place in the closet!" I was laughing and crying at the same time at the irony of the situation.

Just three days before he died, Jack had finished moving the last load of our belongings from town to the farm, and the check for the sale of the building was deposited into our bank account. Jack had been looking forward to getting a new vehicle once the store sale had gone through. Thanks to a problem with his truck, he had the pleasure of driving a new rented van for the last week of his life. He even had all of his laundry up-to-date because we went to the laundromat in the morning on the Monday that he died.

I remember the beautiful smile of contentment on his face as we arrived at the laundromat. He had a habit of bringing his electric razor with him and plugging it into the receptacle in the washroom there. With no power at home, he used about two minutes of their power to give himself a quick shave. He remarked to me that if they had a coin-operated shower for us to use while our laundry was spinning around in the washers, we would have all that we needed until we got those facilities at our farm. The coffee shop was next door and we had a chance to visit over coffee while our clothes were washing. There was a grocery store and a drug store in the same shopping center, so we could pick up anything we needed all at the same time.

On my first birthday without Jack, I was looking out the window and saw a blue butterfly cross in front of where I was watching. It was the earliest I had ever seen one of them and I took it as a special birthday present sent to me from my husband in Heaven. He knew how much those blue butterflies meant to me ever since that first summer of owning the farm when I spotted them. I had never seen blue butterflies before, and I took them as a sign from Heaven that our farm was special.

I knew that Jack would have planned a birthday party for me this year, as it was my sixtieth. For this reason, I gave myself a gathering to begin the work on my dream of a chapel in the woods. I didn't tell those who had volunteered to help me that it was my birthday but asked them to stay for supper. Four energetic seniors, Lilias, Tom, Roy and Rachel, joined me and we began the cleanup, raking around the outside of the building, and hauling away some of the debris. In anticipation of a large gathering, I had called the mini-mart for four chickens, made myself a carrot cake (Jack didn't eat carrot cake), and we ended up serving supper to seventeen guests. One of those friends, Paul Clarke, showed such an interest in the chapel project that he was soon enlisted as the chairman of the building committee. He and his wife, Denise, spent many hours at Jack's Farm this past summer. Paul probably gave our chapel, christened "Casa Maria," more hours than his family cottage up north, but without him and his many assistants, there was no hope of getting the dream project underway. Tim "the book man" Julien had not left yet for Down Under, so he worked side by side with Paul for hours, taking a special interest in the project.

Jennifer came out two mornings that first week at eight o'clock, and using a crow bar, took out the balance of the attached shed at the back of the "little house," as Jack used to call it. She works and lives almost an hour away, so she had to make a two-hour round trip to donate just two hours of hard labor. That is a dedicated friendship.

About twenty people of different faiths joined forces to renovate this former hired man's house, and they attended the first mass and blessing, which was celebrated on August 22, 2004, by Monsignor Tom Raby. In his homily, this same priest who had blessed our twenty-fifth wedding anniversary, remarked that, "Jack's love for Joan has helped to make her dream come true."

The chapel is not yet complete, but the gift of sharing the farm with others will be enhanced by the visits to the chapel that will be made in the coming years. Jack had promised me that we would begin this project together in the spring, and no doubt he helped to inspire the hearts of those who offered to help. I learned how to drywall mud and have now offered to help my son with the finishing of the kitchen and bathroom in the house, which still require some semi-professional mud work.

John will always remember the day he donated time away from the house renovation to assist the chapel crew. It was the day before his first Father's Day as a new dad, and the first celebration without his own father. He pulled the boards from one of the walls being gutted and found an old tobacco advertisement from a 1950s newspaper. The advertisement showed two fellows, with their shotguns over their shoulders, near a weed bed, probably after a duck hunt, and it read: "Like father...like son. Fathers and sons together enjoy Old Chums mild, mellow flavour..." Neither Jack nor John were smokers, but they *were* duck hunters, and the message seemed so fitting for a Father's Day weekend. We placed this yellowed and tattered paper souvenir in Jack's remembrance book.

At the time of the chapel blessing, our friends Janet and Glen Allingham, who had visited us through a blizzard the previous winter, gave me a hurricane lamp and attached to it the words of King George VI, stated in his Christmas message of December 25, 1939:

I said to a man who stood at the gate of the year, give me a light that I may tread safely into the unknown, and he replied: Go out into the darkness and put your hand into the hand of God, that shall be to you better than light and safer than the known way.

About two weeks after receiving their gift, I was at an auction sale and saw a framed piece of cross-stitch needlepoint with the same quotation. I purchased that cross-stitch because it was confirmation to me again of Jack's departure having been the will of God. Jack began the New Year with much expectation and joy that our future was now secure. I like to believe that he died content in the knowledge that his work on earth had been achieved and the love he left behind was enough to sustain us.

C. S. Lewis wrote a book, entitled *A Grief Observed,* about his pain on losing his wife, Joy, to cancer. When he discussed the loss of her physical presence, he indicated that he expected that her spirit would grow more obvious and be of comfort to him. He was a man of strong faith and assumed that this would help him to feel Joy's presence near him. What he soon learned was that as long as he was overwhelmed with the pain of his grief, her spirit was not revealed. As the grief began to heal, he could feel her spirit growing closer and stronger.

I understand what he meant because I, too, have experienced the comfort of my husband's spirit. And, like Lewis, I couldn't dream about him or sense his nearness in the early stages of the grieving process.

Of course, I didn't expect a visitation from Jack in a ghost-like sense. I just wanted a few "real as life" dreams where he might curl up beside me and hold me one more time. That didn't happen. Once I caught a glimpse of him walking through a room, but he didn't seem to recognize me. I didn't like that dream. In one year, I have only felt his presence during one beautiful dream where I sensed he was in the same room, and I awoke feeling satisfied and stronger. I am sure that Jack's spirit broke through the veil that night.

Our daughter Lisa told me that about a week after her father's passing, she dreamt about him. In her dream, he was wearing his favorite red plaid shirt and jeans, and he was running. She caught up with him and had to tackle him to the ground, saying, "Dad, it's you!" He smiled and said to her, "I love it here."

Jack is free now. I know that his spirit is everywhere I look here at the farm. Little reminders are important. The other morning I reached into the kitchen cupboard for a cup for my tea and spotted Jack's mug. His favorite mug that he used each day is brown with small white polka dots and a wide handle that he said fit his hand the best. I used to be so afraid to break this mug because it is thirty years old. Now I have a quiet cup of tea in it every once in awhile, and remember him sipping coffee from it. I bought two of them at the time for fifty cents each, but we never found another mug all of those years that had the same style of handle. I found it ironic that the mug outlasted Jack. I had worried about breaking it for nothing.

Now, when I do the laundry, there are still a few pairs of his Happy Foot socks and plaid shirts spinning together with my clothes. I find this comforting, and although his shirts don't quite close over my full-figured front, they are cosy and comforting to my lonely heart.

On certain occasions, like driving by St. James Cemetery, which I do quite often as it is nearby, I might say hello or I love you. I speak the words out loud and feel a strength and closeness in believing that he hears me say them. Whenever I am overtired, I pray for strength, and I am sure that he sees me, and also prays for me.

I have not taken off my wedding rings. I asked a few other widows about what I should do, and learned that there are two schools of thought, both of which are acceptable. I loved being Mrs. Jack Earle and I feel that I still am this person. Yes, he is not physically present in my life, but the love we shared remains in my heart and all around me.

When I was in my early twenties, I remember hearing someone older and wiser say that all we ever really leave behind us when we pass from this world is love. If we truly share what talents we have, care about the needs of others and try our best each day, then there will be a bounty of lasting love left behind for others to treasure. There is a new adventure forming in my life—a depth of spirit, which I have never known, an abundance of grace, a sense of angelic protection, and peace in the midst of my sorrow. Jack's legacy is overflowing.

Epilogue
Valentine's Day 2005

Life is constantly changing. We know that tomorrow will be very different from today and we can never return to yesterday. Things around Jack's Farm have also changed, and in some ways, for the better.

There are hydro poles now that have altered the look of the fields that border my road. They arrived in the late summer of 2004, and although it was extremely costly to bring power to the farm, it was a necessity in order to upgrade my pioneer lifestyle. First the power, then the power runs the pump to pump the water from the well. A septic bed is created, the pipes for the plumbing arrive, and the outhouse is retired. As of this writing, a flush toilet is just a few weeks away. There are shiny new taps in the kitchen, offering me hope that running water is imminent.

"There is no real hurry," I told my son John, who is saving his mother a lot of money by doing many of the inside renovations. "I survived a cold winter without indoor plumbing last year, and I can do it again." By next winter, I am sure I will have the luxury of a toilet, a shower and the joy of washing dishes in a real sink.

Another of the changes that came about in the year following Jack's death was the closing of the antique store in the little white church. Our friends Rick and Lorraine decided to sell their building as they now plan to run their business from their home. They still don't seem to mind my calling and offering to trade them a loaf of my homemade bread for a shower.

Our cat, Sammy, disappeared in August. We are assuming that a fisher may have taken him. For weeks, with Jessie at my side, I called his name from the front door, but he never returned. I expect that Jack now has the pleasure of his company in Heaven.

I used to get to sleep more easily but now that I have power, I also have television. With my rabbit ears, I can bring in at least three stations and sometimes find myself so captivated by the new "forensic" programs that I am waking up with the odd nightmare. I will have to learn to discipline my viewing to shows that are less stimulating. Before television, my battery-operated radio lulled me to sleep with classical music.

My memories of Jack are growing stronger and more precious. It is true that once the healing process begins, our hearts are open again to celebrate the little things that grief had clouded from our minds.

My granddaughter Arianna, who is fifteen months old, reached out her arms to me for the first time recently, inviting me to pick her up. This was a new connection for us and my heart sang with the awareness that I might no longer be Jack's wife, but

I was her grandmother, and when her beautiful dark eyes look at me with love, they will remind me of her Grampa Jack and his eyes that were full of love for me.

Acknowledgments

Gail Baird, the publisher of this book, came into my life 11 years ago when I sent her a manuscript I had written. She rejected that book, but responded with an encouraging letter that made me feel that I should keep on writing. Five years later, I sent her another manuscript, and this time she gave the proposal a very serious look but graciously told me that she felt it was not a project she could take on. The third time, I offered her this manuscript. This time, "deeply moved" by the story of Jack's Farm, she took the leap of faith and offered to publish it.

I am grateful for the confidence she has placed in me and I appreciate the integrity and style that have been a part of the preparation of this book.

To all my friends, those mentioned and those in the background, who have always supported my dreams, thank you for caring and sharing. To Lisa Dawn and John and Sarah, Dad is very proud of all that you are doing to help with the farm. To my parents, who continue to believe in my ability, I am who I am because of your influence.

About the Author

For 15 years, Joan Levy Earle and husband Jack Earle owned and operated The Sanctuary, a book and stationery store, situated in the historic Kyte Building in Cornwall, Ontario.

Joan's first career involved teaching her unique style of baton twirling in Scarborough, Alexandria and Cornwall. Over the years, she encouraged hundreds of young ladies to develop their poise and confidence in the majorette schools that she founded.

Joan is an accomplished painter in oils, with subject matter ranging from landscapes to spiritual pieces, and her work is currently represented in Kingston, Ontario, at the Agnes Etherington Gallery.

The most poignant and personal of Joan's published works, *Jack's Farm* is the author's eighth book. She is a regular contributor to the *Sacred Heart Messenger* magazine, and to Cornwall's *Standard Freeholder,* where her "Hopelines" column has been a popular weekly feature for many years.

We would love to hear your thoughts on *Jack's Farm.*

Please visit us on-line at www.jacksfarm.ca, where you will find:

- Discussion questions for Book Clubs
- Multiple-copy order discounts
- Pictures of Jack's Farm
- Send comments or a review
- What other readers are saying
- Other books by Creative Bound

Jack's Farm
Joan Levy Earle